MAGDA ROMANSKA

# DIGITAL ACCESS TO THE PERFORMING ARTS

## Comparative Study of Legal and Structural Challenges

BRISTOL
UNIVERSITY
PRESS

First published in Great Britain in 2026 by

Bristol University Press
University of Bristol
1-9 Old Park Hill
Bristol
BS2 8BB
UK
t: +44 (0)117 374 6645
e: bup-info@bristol.ac.uk

Details of international sales and distribution partners are available at bristoluniversitypress.co.uk



DOI: 10.51952/9781529257052



British Library Cataloguing in Publication Data
A catalogue record for this book is available from the British Library

ISBN 978-1-5292-5703-8 hardcover
ISBN 978-1-5292-5704-5 ePub
ISBN 978-1-5292-5705-2 OA Pdf



Cover design: blu inc
Front cover image: iStock/3DSculptor
Bristol University Press uses environmentally responsible print partners.
Printed and bound in Great Britain by CPI Group (UK) Ltd, Croydon, CR0 4YY

Bristol University Press' authorised representative in the European Union is: Easy Access System Europe, Mustamäe tee 50, 10621 Tallinn, Estonia,
Email: gpsr.requests@easproject.com

FSC
www.fsc.org
MIX
Paper | Supporting responsible forestry
FSC® C013604

# Contents

# Acknowledgements

This study was developed by the selected members of the Digital Access Research Project at metaLAB (at) Harvard. It focuses on the digital accessibility of performing arts, new developing strategies for improved copyright content management, and the codification of streaming as part of disability laws in the US and globally. It provides a comparative analysis of digital accessibility in performing arts across four regulatory frameworks: the United States, United Kingdom, European Union, and Australia, highlighting legal and structural challenges to digital access and addressing potential avenues of improvements. The COVID-19 pandemic accelerated digital pivoting in performing arts, revealing both opportunities and obstacles. Data from the four regions indicates similar trends: increased digital programming led to greater participation by the people with disabilities, elderly, and younger diverse audiences, yet often failed to deliver expected economic benefits to performing arts institutions. The assumption that digital programming needed to be self-sustaining (unlike subsidized in-person programming) has led to widespread elimination of online offerings, reverting to pre-pandemic exclusion of previously neglected audiences. This study highlights the complex interplay between copyright laws, disability rights, and human rights to culture, advocating for a paradigm shift that would prioritize accessibility. It recommends developing international legal guidelines, expanding copyright exceptions, and fostering collaborations between theatres and tech companies to ensure sustainable digital access. The study emphasizes the urgent need to reconcile artists' rights with the civil rights of disabled and marginalized audiences, proposing that digital access to performing arts should be considered an essential component of cultural accessibility, codified in a variety of international and national laws.

This project would not be possible without the support of the Berkman Klein Center for Internet and Society at Harvard Law School and metaLAB (at) Harvard. Special thanks should be extended to my colleagues, Jeffrey Schnapp, Lins Derry, and Sarah Newman, for their steadfast encouragement and support, and to Rebecca Tabasky, whose early comments and suggestions have been invaluable in launching this project. Deep gratitude and debt are owed to the members of our Digital Access Research Project, who contributed sections to this book, offered feedback, and shared their research, especially Maxime de Brogniez, Paul Harpur, Ioan Kaes, Kasia Lech, Richard Misek, Jessica Rizzo, Ilinca Todorut, Antoine Vandenbulke, Jim Augustine, David Ball, Doug Reside, and Heidi Wiley. The support of others, Christopher T. Bavitz, Steven Chaikelson, Sam Gold, and Ramona Mosse, is also greatly appreciated. Finally, my heartfelt thanks goes to my assistant Kate Luhr, and to Emerson College for its institutional support.

# Digital Access Research Project (DARP) Members

**Magda Romanska**, Chair of the DARP; Faculty Associate at Berkman Klein Center for Internet and Society at Harvard; Professor of Performing Arts at Emerson College, Boston, MA; and Researcher at metaLAB (at) Harvard.

**Jim Augustine**, former COO of Zuckerberg Media, co-founder of Assemble Stream; co-founder of the League of Live Stream Theater.

**Christopher T. Bavitz**, Wilmer Hale Clinical Professor of Law and Managing Director at Cyberlaw Clinic at the Berkman Klein Center for Internet and Society at Harvard.

**Maxime de Brogniez**, Lawyer and Lecturer of Law at University of Liège, Belgium.

**Steven Chaikelson**, Professor of Professional Practice in Theatre at Columbia University School of the Arts and Adjunct Professor at Columbia Law School at Columbia University, NYC.

**Gregory Dorchak**, Assistant Attorney, US Department of Justice, Civil Rights Unit.

**Sam Gold**, Theatre Director, NYC.

**Paul Harpur**, Professor of Law at The University of Queensland Law School, Australia; Affiliate Researcher at The Harvard Law School Project on Disability.

**Ioan Kaes**, General Secretary at AEPO-ARTIS.

**Kasia Lech**, Associate Professor of Global Theatre History at the University of Amsterdam; Executive Director of TheTheatreTimes.com; Affiliate at metaLAB (at) Harvard.

**Richard Misek**, Professor at the University of Bergen, Norway; Principal Investigator of *Digital Access to Arts and Culture in U.K.*

**Ramona Mosse**, Head of Theatre at the Zurich University of the Arts, Switzerland; Research Affiliate at metaLAB (at) Harvard.

**Faith Obafemi**, Lawyer and Tech Policy Analyst, Co-Founder, Head of Strategy, Future-Proof Intelligence at Kleros.

**Doug Reside**, Curator, Theatre Collection, New York Public Library, NYC.

**Jessica Rizzo**, Attorney, Ballard Spahr LLP, Philadelphia, DFA Yale School of Drama.

**Talia Rodgers**, Head of Higher Education, DigitalTheatre.com.

**Maitreya Shah**, Fellow, Berkman Klein Center for Internet and Society at Harvard.

**Ilinca Todorut**, Faculty of Theatre and Film at Babeș-Bolyai University in Romania; Artistic Director of the International Online Theatre Festival (IOTF); Affiliate at metaLAB (at) Harvard.

**Antoine Vandenbulke**, Professor of Law at the School of Law of the University of Mons – Free University of Brussels, Belgium.

**Heidi Wiley**, Executive Director of European Theatre Convention (ETC).

# ONE

# Introduction

The New York Public Library for the Performing Arts has permission from the Broadway Unions and Guilds to record, store, and share videos of live theatre productions within the confines of the Library archives, under strict guidelines and staff supervision. When patrons who are disabled, elderly, or ill cannot physically come to the Library, are NYPL staff obliged to follow the contracts the institution has with the unions, or is the Library obliged to follow American with Disabilities Act laws and provide such patrons with digital access to the archive without the need to ask permission from the unions? What is the legal status of the digital performance texts, both archived and newly made, when the rights of the copyright holders conflict with the civil rights of the people with disabilities?[1]

Digital access to performing arts is fraught with many such complex legal questions and logistical challenges. Which laws – the copyright and contract laws protecting the rights of the artists, or the civil rights of the people with disabilities – should take precedence when the person with the disability is unable to access the art event, whether live or recorded, in person? Is digital access to performing arts part of the standard accessibility package that theatres and other performing arts institutions should offer to their homebound, geographically distant, disabled, ill, and elderly patrons? In his article 'Disability and Copyright', legal scholar Blake Reid notes that although copyright laws have impeded access to a wide range of media for people with disabilities, it is an issue that has received limited attention from legal scholars and activists.[2] Reid writes:

> A vast array of copyrighted works – books, video programming, software, podcasts, video games, and more – remain inaccessible to people with disabilities. International efforts to adopt limitations and exceptions to copyright law that permit third parties to create and distribute accessible versions of books for people with print disabilities have drawn some attention to the role that copyright law plays in inhibiting the accessibility of copyrighted works. However, copyright scholars have not meaningfully engaged with the role that copyright law plays in the broader tangle of disability rights.[3]

This study attempts to fill the gap between disability rights and copyright scholarship by presenting a comparative analysis of the state of digital accessibility of the performing arts in the US, the UK, European Union, and Australia, highlighting the legal and structural challenges to digital access, and addressing potential avenues for improvements. Moreover, while the core challenge lies in reconciling copyright and disability laws, additional considerations include: adapting legal frameworks for new digital formats, ensuring access for research purposes, and preserving materials through archivization (for both historical documentation and AI datasets).

Although legal and funding models differ from country to country, a combination of structural and legal factors continues to make access to the performing arts inaccessible to many disabled and marginalized audiences, despite what seemed like an overnight explosion of online programming during the global COVID-19 lockdowns. Ironically, the pandemic revealed the enormous disparity in access to the performing arts, particularly as the majority of institutions either curtailed or completely shut down the streaming divisions they had developed during the lockdowns once the governments around the world declared the 'return to normal'. With this return – or regression – theatres once again began actively excluding disabled and marginalized audiences, who by then had begun treating digital access as an integral component of performing arts programming.

## Performance is a human right

According to Article 27 of the Universal Declaration of Human Rights (UDHR), adopted by the United Nations General Assembly in 1948, 'the right to take part in cultural life guarantees the right of everyone to access, participate in and enjoy culture, cultural heritage and cultural expressions'.[4] Ratified by 173 countries and part of the International Covenant on Civil and Political Rights, Article 27 also proclaims that everyone has the right 'to enjoy their own culture'.[5] Furthermore, Article 15 of the International Covenant on Economic, Social and Cultural Rights, adopted in 1966 and ratified by 172 countries of the General Assembly, includes the right 'to take part in cultural life' of one's country as fundamental.[6]

The United Nations considers access to culture to be so essential that its *Convention on the Rights of Persons with Disabilities* (resolution 61/106 adopted on 24 January 2007) makes special provision for exceptions to intellectual property rights to account for the accessibility needs of the people with disabilities: 'States Parties shall take all appropriate steps, in accordance with international law, to ensure that laws protecting intellectual property rights do not constitute an unreasonable or discriminatory barrier to access by persons with disabilities to cultural materials.'[7] However, while the *Convention* acknowledges the potential conflict between copyright laws and the rights of the people with disabilities, it falls short in providing pragmatic solutions on how to resolve this conflict, nor does it exert significant pressure on governments to explicitly address it.[8]

The human right to culture is internationally recognized as vital to public health, with social exclusion carrying significant health risks for all age groups.[9] The 2024 'On the Move' report on cultural mobility, funded by European Union, opened the study noting that:

> Numerous studies and cultural initiatives, at local, national, and European levels, have explored the diverse ways in which the arts and culture contribute to the well-being and overall health, including mental health, of the population. Extensive research has provided robust and tangible evidence of how the sector bolsters the sustainability and resilience of societies, especially when engaging with vulnerable communities.[10]

In addition to benefiting individual health and well-being, access to culture profoundly influences social, political, and economic processes across both national and international scales. In December 2024, The Council of the European Union issued another report, the 'Council Conclusions on Improving and Fostering Access to Culture' (C/2024/7446). The report is yet the most forceful reiteration of 'the importance of cultural participation for personal health, well-being, territorial and societal cohesion, as well as in strengthening democracy'.[11] In addition to reiterating that the right to culture is a human right, the report further stresses the need to acknowledge:

> The intrinsic value of culture as a basis for creativity and self-expression, to support mental health and well-being, and to enhance quality of life. Culture also contributes to local and regional development, innovation, productive entrepreneurship and economic progress by helping people acquire key competences, supporting knowledge-sharing, building self-confidence and empowerment to (re)enter the labour market and equipping people for lifelong learning.[12]

The Report lists an array of obstacles that can prevent a person from accessing culture. The challenges include:

> physical and personal financial limitations; psychological obstacles; sensory, cognitive and cultural barriers; all forms of stereotypes and discriminations including gender; technological obstacles; the lack of accessibility in built and virtual environments, information, communication, products and services; as well as the lack of time and interest. That access to culture is strongly related to levels of education, financial opportunities, inclusion, accessibility, geographical circumstances and health conditions.[13]

Despite all the individual and societal benefits of cultural access, often other, more pressing, life-and-death rights draw more of the international spotlight and inspire more activism, with the right to access cultural life rarely examined or enforced. According to the United Nations Department of Economic and Social Affairs focused on Disability, 'Around 15 per cent of the world's population, or estimated 1 billion people, live with disabilities. They are the world's largest minority.'[14] WHO considers this group among the 'most marginalized groups in the world'.[15] For this largest minority – but also other neglected populations, including the elderly and the clinically vulnerable – as well as other socially and economically excluded and the geographically distant groups, their human right to culture, including to performing arts, is often not just elusive but effectively unreachable. Resolving the complex nexus of copyright, contract laws, performer's rights, funding models, and the human right to culture has become an urgent imperative for culture makers and institutional leaders. This task is particularly pressing now, as new technologies necessitate revision of the current copyright and contract laws related to creative output. 'A consideration of the appropriate L&Es [limitations and exceptions] for persons with disabilities, therefore, lies at the intersection of human rights and IP law and requires the advancement of human rights using copyright's legal and policy mechanisms.'[16] This project attempts to address some of these challenges within the context of performing arts and disability laws across the four aforementioned regulatory regimes: copyright, contract law, performers' rights, and human rights law.

## Project background

In 2021, at the height of the global COVID-19 pandemic, metaLAB (at) Harvard, located at the Berkman Klein Center for Internet and Society at Harvard Law School, brought together a group of artists, researchers, and arts managers to discuss, in the span of a few months, the changes in technology and access that the pandemic activated within the performing arts sector around the world. The Future Stage project focused on identifying 'the needs and possibilities for media, culture, and presence in a hyperconnected world; the civic stakes of the performing arts today; the emergent modes and genres of performance and organization; the architecture of future performance spaces; and the future professions that will animate those performance venues'.[17]

The result of these online convenings was the *Future Stage Manifesto*, a working paper that put forth a vision of inclusive, hybrid, transmedial, global performing arts. The *Manifesto*'s key themes included 'performance as a human right, architectures that promote connectivity, expanded concepts of liveness, sustainable models of touring, a rethinking of streaming not as a fallback option but instead as an expressive medium, and the need for new institutional and fiscal models'.[18] The *Manifesto* considered the shifting dynamics between art, technology, and public discourse, accelerated by the advancements in digital and AI integration, and by the demands of the pandemic. It proposed a re-evaluation of liveness, 'Liveness Plus', as a concept historically fundamental to the performing arts, augmented now by new hybrid and digital performances spaces, and new roles for human workers whose creativity would animate them. In response to the climate crisis, the *Manifesto* repositioned physical touring as no longer necessary for the global dissemination of performing arts events. Recognizing the challenges to artistic expression posed by the digital and AI revolutions, the *Manifesto* also put forth the necessity for the artists to 'own the stream', to be the primary beneficiaries of their artistic labour.[19]

In the months following its publication, the *Manifesto* was translated into 13 languages and republished in online publications around the world, eliciting numerous written responses and inspiring conferences, panels, and museum exhibits engaging with its proposals.[20] An interest in the *Manifesto* appears to indicate that the global theatre's community is grappling with the complexity of making theatre in the age of new technology and the challenges to status quo it introduced, including issues of access and copyright.

In 2023, following the worldwide reception of the *Future Stage Manifesto*, metaLAB (at) Harvard launched the Digital Access Research Project (DARP). DARP has continued to pursue the lines of inquiry initiated by the Future Stage project, with a renewed focus on investigating the digital accessibility of performing arts events, developing strategies and methodologies for improved copyright content management, and engineering the codification of streaming as part of the disability laws in the US and globally.

The DARP group consists of leading international experts in disability law, copyright law, digital technology, and performing arts management. The objective of DARP is to develop a set of guidelines for policy makers, lawmakers and performing arts organizations that would balance the digital accessibility needs of the marginalized groups with the rights of the copyright holders. Drawing on research from the EU and the UK on the accessibility implications of online theatre, as well as related requirements regarding authors' rights when broadcasting live performances, the DARP group researches promising practices and replicable strategies for performing arts companies that wish to continue offering events which can be streamed and made available online. This study was developed by the selected group of DARP members in 2023–24 during the year-long process of monthly online meetings and collaborations. It is an attempt to open a debate about the accessibility of performing arts with the *a priori* assumption that prioritizing such access is both legally warranted, politically and socially desirable, and ethically necessary.

# TWO

# Theatre and Digitality

## Before the COVID-19 pandemic

Already long before the COVID-19 pandemic, theatres were experiencing a number of challenges in attracting new audiences. Younger generations could neither afford theatre outings nor considered them more appealing than the variety of streaming services they could easily access from the privacy of their own homes. In her introduction to *The Routledge Companion to Dramaturgy*, published in 2014, Magda Romanska pointed out that theatres have mostly been ignoring these emerging challenges to fill the seats and are not prepared to face the generational shift in audience habits, often dismissing the emerging digital technologies that have potential to alter both theatre-making and theatre-viewing practices:

> The changing makeup of American audiences will eventually force all theatres to restructure their season-planning practices, as will the emergence of new technologies that are altering our theatre-going habits. With Netflix, YouTube, and other internet services providing any type of entertainment on demand, in the privacy of one's own home, the ritual of going to the theatre is becoming increasingly endangered. In the December 2013 issue of *The Wall Street Journal*, drama critic Terry Teachout observes: 'The idea that you might voluntarily go out at night to see a half-dozen human beings act out a story in person … is now alien

> to most Americans, especially younger ones.'[1] If it is to survive these two major paradigm shifts (the changes in population and the emergence of new streaming technologies), American theatre needs dramaturgical leadership to both broaden and maintain its audience base. New collaborative technologies, peer-to-peer exchange platforms, and user-driven feedback create new opportunities for virtual literary office management that can change our season-planning practices. … It is up to the dramaturgical field at large to see how to use the new technology to remain relevant and to advance the practice of theatre in the most inclusive way.[2]

Research studies confirmed these observations and the need for broader digital engagement. In 2024, the US-based Wallace Foundation released a multiyear study on audience development. Titled 'In Search of a Magic Bullet: Results from the Building Audiences for Sustainability Initiative', the study was conducted in response to a 2015 NEA report on the alarming rate of decline in American theatre audiences.[3] It included a data-driven analysis of different audience development strategies implemented by 25 large performing arts organizations, with the majority of surveys concluded in 2019, before the COVID-19 pandemic began (*Building Audiences for Sustainability* (BAS) 2015 to 2019 initiative). Since theatres were already struggling to fill in the seats, they agreed to experiment with a variety of audience-building approaches. The Wallace Foundation research project aimed to evaluate and quantify the long-term effectiveness of these approaches.

Some strategies, like 'crossover programming', meaning 'special programming [offered] to attract the target audience, in the hopes that the target audience would then cross over and attend [the organization's] main programs', failed to deliver anticipated audience expansion. Other approaches, particularly increased implementation of robust digital communications and marketing (email, social media networks, short video releases) aimed at educating audiences about the theatres' offerings, did provide more desirable results, bringing in new audience members.[4]

Prior to the pandemic, the majority of mainstream theatre and performing arts organizations remained hesitant to embrace digital culture and the potential for experimentation and audience outreach it offered. This reluctance persisted even as they faced challenges to audience expansion for in-person programming, now in competition with at-home streaming services, and despite the impact that effective digital communication could have on their bottom line. There was scepticism about the digital tools, concern over the implementation cost, and lack of in-house technological expertise.

In opposition to mainstream organizations, however, the pre-pandemic fringe and avant-garde segment of the performing arts did engage with the increased digitalization of our public sphere, producing a broad range of cutting-edge, web-based interactive theatre experiments, including but not limited to podplays and other sonic performance experiments (sound games, sound walks, immersive soundscapes), network plays (works of theatre written in blockchain or navigated through on YouTube, or scripted performances which unfold live via text or on platforms like Facebook, Twitter, or Instagram), robo- and data plays (algorithmic performances, technobjects, and data-based dramaturgies), Virtual Reality (VR) and Augmented Reality (AR) plays (video game plays, performances on Second Life, hybrid performances which combine VR or AR and live and online interaction), and other interactive, new media-based theatre and performance projects.

Avant-garde artists experimented with a variety of digital formats, from Twitter plays like Jeremy Gable's *The 15th Line* (2010) to interactive fiction video games such as Emily Short's award-winning *Galatea* (2010). Some other early examples of digital theatre experiments include the BBC and Arts Council England's project, *The Space*, which opened in 2014 with a crowdsourced hackathon in Tate Modern's Turbine Hall. The same year, the Barbican in the UK created *The Digital Revolution: An Immersive Exhibition of Art, Design, Film, Music and Video Games*. It was described as 'the most comprehensive presentation of digital creativity ever to be staged in the UK'.[5]

Also in 2014, the London International Festival of Theatre (LIFT) streamed Elastic Future's *Longitude*, and Blast Theory developed the live/online chase game *I'd Hide You*.[6] In 2015, Christina Papagiannouli, who directs and devises cyberformances on online platforms such as UpStage and Waterwheel Tap, published her monograph *Political Cyberformance: The Etheatre Project*.[7] In 2017, IJAD Dance Company launched its pioneering digital platform, the Open Online Theatre, with the world premiere of *Walk Into Space*, 'an interactive, dance extravaganza exploring gravity and the wonders of the universe'.[8]

In the world of academic scholarship, research on the role of new technologies in multimedia performance has proliferated since the mid-2000s, though it has not yet at this time focused on online and hybrid works. In 2007, Steve Dixon published *Digital Performance: A History of New Media in Theatre, Dance, Performance Art, and Installation*, and in 2010, Chris Salter published *Entangled: Technology and the Transformation of Performance*. In 2010, Sarah Bay-Cheng, with a group of editors, published an edited collection, *Mapping Intermediality in Performance*. Also in 2010, *The International Journal of Performance Arts and Digital Media* was founded to provide a venue for the publication of a growing body of interdisciplinary academic research on the subject of theatre and digitality. In 2014, *The Routledge Companion to Dramaturgy* published a number of articles on the use of digital technologies in multiplatform environments, including Second Life plays and social media.[9] And in 2015, Sarah Bay-Cheng, Jen Parker-Starbuck, and Chris Saltz published another collection, *Performance and Media: Taxonomies for a Changing Field*. In 2016, *Theatre*, Yale's journal of plays, criticism, and reportage, launched its special issue on 'Digital Feelings' (*Theatre* 46, no. 2[10]), a sequel to the 2012 explorations of 'Digital Dramaturgies' (*Theatre* 42, no. 2), which focused on the intersection of performance and digital technologies. In 'Digital Feelings', the editors, Jacob Gallagher-Ross and Miriam Felton-Dansky, asked, 'How does the digital sphere script new emotional experiences or give the old ones a new twist?'[11] The issue showcased a broad range of online performances – Twitter plays and networked performance – and included a script and sampling of code from Andrew Schneider's live-generated, digitally produced monodrama, *YOUARENOWHERE.*[12] In 2023 Joanna Tompkins's article on 'The Digital Turn', published in the *Theatre Journal*, outlined the history of research on digital theatre during the prior decade.[13]

Simultaneously in Europe, in 2019, right before the COVID-19 pandemic, the European Commission's project Culture for the Future, which was part of the international colloquium held in Brussels in June of the same year, issued several recommendations, including with regard to 'access to cultural diversity and visibility of diverse cultural content in the digital environment'. The culture of the future, the Commission asserted, must:

> Ensure balanced flows of digital cultural goods and services and recognize their public value and specific nature, based on their cultural, social and economic dimensions.
>
> Improve the collective bargaining position of creators for the rights of their works and promote dialogue between online content sharing service providers and right holders.
>
> Raise awareness about the functioning of the digital cultural environment by investing in research and knowledge institutions and networks.[14]

While digital culture was becoming part of the experimental performing arts scene, and the importance of digital culture was slowly gaining recognition as part of diversification efforts, digitality was not yet part of the broader international or national discourse on performing arts access. It was not considered a standard element of accessible programming. There was also no data available on the participation in the performing arts of the marginalized audiences: disabled, elders, the clinically vulnerable, the socially and economically excluded, and the geographically distant. It was assumed that they would either somehow manage to get themselves to the theatre or they would simply not come. They were not considered an audience valuable enough to pursue or research.

## Performing arts during the COVID-19 pandemic lockdowns

The 2024 report by the Societies and Cultures Institute at Exeter University, 'Pandemic Preparedness in the Live Performing Arts', noted that 'Digital emerged during the pandemic as a means of continuing creative programme delivery and outreach during lockdown, an opportunity for e-commerce, and as a fundraising tool'.[15] The report points out that while the pandemic presented an opportunity for expanded digital access, it also 'exposed low levels of digital capacity in the performing arts sector and a scarcity of technical skills training and soft digital transferrable skills'.[16] The pandemic lockdowns affected the entire performing arts sector: 'At the start of the pandemic, commercial and subsidized theatres alike struggled with being officially open while audiences were advised not to attend.'[17]

Nonetheless, despite these challenges, theatres worldwide produced an impressive array of online and hybrid programming during the COVID-19 pandemic lockdowns. Many theatres either livestreamed their shows, made older archival productions available online, or created brand new, hybrid, transmedial, and digital works that straddled the line between live and digital theatre-making. While the closures of performance venues were devastating to many theatre artists and smaller institutions, and it will take years for some of the local theatre ecosystems to recover and adapt to the post-COVID-19 world, it also spurred unprecedented innovation. Unable to mount traditional in-person, live performances, many theatre artists embraced the live and interactive online shows using a variety of interactive technologies and formats, including teleconferencing, video games, VR, AR, haptic technologies, social media, and phone and text messaging. The pandemic fostered an incredible outpouring of creativity and cutting-edge, intermedial and transmedial experiments. Although it predated the pandemic, the nascent artistic form flourished during the lockdowns; variously called digital theatre, transmedia theatre, hybrid theatre, or cyber theatre, it blended theatre with film, video game, augmented reality, and teleconferencing.

For many disabled theatre artists and audiences, this outpouring of online experiments meant far greater access to the performing arts than before the pandemic, in the form of streamed old or new shows, participation in online workshops and rehearsals, and a variety of interactive and hybrid performance models.[18] Digital access suddenly made performing arts available to broader, previously underserved audiences, including people with disabilities, elderly, and the clinically vulnerable, but also the socially and economically excluded and the geographically distant. As a result of this increased digital availability of performing arts, formerly neglected participants, both artists and audiences, came to see the provision of online performing arts as an essential accessibility feature. This digital pivot, as the Exeter University report notes,

> opened doors for previously excluded practitioners and audiences … People of colour participated more in digital events … Disabled audiences and practitioners benefited from digital access, as did people with mental health conditions during the first lockdown. … Digital increased the visibility of attempts to engage young

> people in theatre, with younger viewers preferring on-demand content. ... There was a drop in engagement levels with culture for older people, but older audiences did engage with streamed or recorded live performance, expanding demographic and geographical reach.[19]

This report highlights that the benefits of new digital access extended new and unexpected advantages beyond accessibility, such as improved life-work balance for theatre workers and a more ecologically conscious approach to the theatre-making process itself. The report goes so far as to suggest that the inclusion of modern technologies held promise of solving a variety of problems plaguing the theatre industry:

> Some workers within the theatre industry who remained in work reported positive impacts resulting from working from home and the pivot to digital; this brought about some flexibility, wellbeing and inclusion benefits along with new opportunities and income streams. Creative freelancers turned to online spaces and platforms for support. Continuing to work required a great deal of adaptability and multi-tasking. There is evidence of widespread upskilling in digital working methods and some inclusion benefits resulting from self-taped auditions. ... Digital created opportunities for more ecologically mindful performance and rehearsal practices involving telepresence technologies that reduced the need to travel and enabled some cost savings even as at the high end of digital production, costs could be prohibitive. Digital performance was therefore identified as having the potential to solve some long-standing problems in the industry.[20]

Overall, however, despite these many documented benefits of the digital pivot, the data from the four regions, United States, United Kingdom, European Union, and Australia, indicate similar trends during and after the pandemic: increased digital programming lead to increased participation in the performing arts by people with disabilities, elder, and younger, more diverse audiences, which nonetheless more often than not and for a variety of reasons failed to deliver the expected economic outcomes to the performing arts institutions, leading to closures and elimination of their online offerings, and thus, the return to the pre-pandemic exclusion of the formerly neglected audiences whom such access benefited the most.

### United States

In March 2021, *American Theatre*, a publication of the Theatre Communication Group (TCG), published an article calling for the codification of the pandemic accessibility gains into an updated ADA law as it relates to the performing arts.[21] In November of the same year, however, *American Theatre* also published the results of a survey conducted by TCG on the financial viability of the streaming models developed during the pandemic. Sixty-four managing and artistic directors from 64 companies in 25 states responded to the survey, revealing that 'all three categories of digital offerings (pre-recorded in-person, pre-recorded virtual, and live virtual) failed to deliver at the box office'. Many companies 'reported a decrease in revenue of 90 percent or greater'.[22] The decline in revenue was not universal, as some companies exceeded their pre-pandemic revenues after adding a digital streaming component. The most risk-taking, experimental companies managed to create new, innovative digital interactive strategies, expanding their audiences by reaching previously hidden national and international demographics.

By eliminating their newly developed online programming, however, most theatres appeared to act against the data on online viewership, as available survey reports on art participation during and after the COVID-19 pandemic indicate a significant growth potential for both livestreamed and archived performing arts events, particularly among younger and more diverse audiences. In October 2023, the National Endowment for the Arts released two reports: 'Arts Attendance and Reading Trends, by Demographic Group: Tables for 2017 and 2022',[23] and 'Online Audiences for Arts Programming: A Survey of Virtual Participation amid COVID-19'.[24] The first report notes 'the overall decline in visual and performing arts [in person] attendance'.[25] At the same time, from 2017 to 2022,

> digital or virtual consumption of art ... can be said to have prospered. As in 2017, this mode of arts participation was easily the most popular among U.S. adults. [F]ar and away the largest share of adults who participated in the arts did so through electronic or digital media (75 percent).[26]

By contrast, only 48 per cent of adults attended art events in person. From 2017 to 2022, the in-person attendance at theatre plays declined by 52 per cent, for musical plays by 38 per cent and for operas by 68 per cent.[27]

The second report focuses specifically on digital arts activities during the COVID-19 pandemic. The report reveals that, overall, in 2022, 69 per cent of surveyed adults viewed archived performing arts events online, and 43 per cent participated in livestreamed performing arts events.[28] In terms of age distribution, survey data indicates greater involvement with digital art among young people:

> Most respondents across all age groups reported doing one or more digital arts activity in the last year. However, younger adults tended to report higher rates of engaging with digital arts activities – 95 percent of 18- to 24-year-olds, compared to 68 percent of people aged 75 and older. ... Eighty percent of younger adults (18- to 24-year-olds) reported watching archived events, while 59 percent of adults aged 65 or older reported doing this activity.[29]

The data also indicates that audiences watching online performing arts events were more diverse than typical audiences for in-person events: 'Of the 43 percent of total respondents who viewed *livestreamed* performing arts events, 65 percent were Black/African American and 45 percent were Hispanic. Only 39 percent of White respondents reported watching livestreamed events.'[30] Similar data is reflected in watching of *archived* performing arts events:

> Black/African American respondents viewed these events at a much higher rate (81 percent) than did White respondents (64 percent). Additionally, 73 percent of Hispanic respondents reported viewing archived performing arts events. In contrast, the trend was reversed for in-person events: 52 percent of White respondents reported attending in-person performing arts events, versus 34 percent of Black/African American respondents.[31]

Overall, 16 per cent of surveyed adults reported attending, viewing, or listening to livestreamed arts events more often in 2022 relative to when the COVID-19 pandemic began, and 13 per cent reported viewing more archived online performing arts events. Thirty-six per cent reported viewing the same number of livestreamed events, and 49 per cent reported viewing the same number of archived events:

> When asked to consider their present-day activities in relation to the first year of the pandemic, higher shares of respondents reported watching or listening to livestreamed or archived performing arts events more often than they reported participating in other virtual arts activities. Further, although 28 percent of respondents reported attending in-person performing arts events more often than in the first year of the pandemic, digital consumption of performing arts also did not diminish – 52 percent

> of all respondents reported watching or listening to livestreamed performing arts events either more often or at the same rate, and 62 percent reported watching or listening to archived livestreamed events more often or at the same rate.[32]

Whereas the participation in livestreamed performing arts events declined in 2022 relative to the first year of the pandemic, the viewing of archived performing arts events declined less among 18–24 years olds (9 per cent vs 7 per cent of all respondents) and increased in the 35–44 age group (31 per cent vs 16 per cent of all respondents). The viewership of livestreamed performing arts events in 2022, relative to the first year of the pandemic, increased among non-White groups:

> 36 percent of Black/African American and 22 percent of Hispanic respondents reported consuming more livestreamed performing arts than in the first year of COVID-19 (compared to 12 percent of White respondents). Similarly, 21 percent of Black/African American respondents reported more often viewing archived livestreamed performing arts events (compared to 11 percent of White respondents).[33]

Overall, the second report highlights that '82 percent of respondents participated in some type of digital arts activity between 2021 and 2022. This figure is roughly comparable to the 75 percent of adults reporting engagement with digital arts activities in the NEA's 2022 Survey of Public Participation in the Arts'.[34] Moreover, 'The GSS survey results suggest that even as the world started to return to in-person activities, digital engagement remained high. Roughly 30 percent of respondents reported doing one or more digital arts activities more often than in the first year of the pandemic.'[35]

Together, the two reports indicate a post-pandemic increase of participation in both livestreamed and archived online performing arts events, relative to before the COVID-19 pandemic, with largest increases among the younger and more diverse audiences. The surveys' data suggest an increased demand for such programming, which seems to run counter to many theatres' rapid return to exclusively in-person seasons when theatres finally opened, while shutting down their digital programmes developed during the pandemic lockdowns.

### *United Kingdom*

Both the UK and the EU funded extensive studies on theatre and digitality during the COVID-19 pandemic, and the results of these surveys are very comparable to those conducted in the US. In 2022, the Arts and Humanities Research Council in the UK released a report on 'Digital Access to Arts and Culture (DAAC)':

> The final report summarizes an 18-month research project into the role of digital arts and culture in the UK during the pandemic, focusing on its accessibility implications. The report pays particular attention to the 'pivot' to online programming undertaken by many arts and culture organizations following the onset of COVID-19. It also explores how online and live programmes have interacted with each other, how digital accessibility tools are finding their way back into in-person activities, and what the wider accessibility implications of the on-going hybridization of arts and culture may be.[36]

The report's authors conclude by arguing that 'hybrid (in-person and online) programming must form a key factor in future accessibility improvements: the more routes that exist for engaging with arts and culture, the easier it is to engage with, and the more inclusive it can become'.[37] The DAAC report stipulates that 'online content is itself an accessibility feature' and should be codified within the existing disability access laws: 'Despite strongly voiced concerns by many d/Deaf, disabled and vulnerable participants in particular, many of the institutional barriers to access that were lowered during the pandemic by online provision have returned.'[38]

The DAAC report also includes a series of recommendations, highlighting the universal accessibility of online streaming as well as the earnings potential for performing arts organizations who chose to develop strong online programming. Furthermore, the authors assert that 'hybrid programming has the potential to achieve broader inclusion goals'.[39] They note that 'online participants are younger and more ethnically diverse than in-person visitors, which suggests huge potential for digital tools to engage new and more diverse participants'.[40] The increased digital access had an impact not only on the disabled audiences but also on ethnic minorities (excluding white minorities), which were 'more likely than white participants to participate subsequently in arts and culture, both digitally and in person'.[41] The authors point out that 'the pandemic has revealed barriers to engagement for many people previously not perceived as having accessibility requirements'.[42]

The 2022 survey report released by the University of Essex, 'Theatres Beyond the Stage: The Recovery of Regional Theatres as Placemakers in the East of England', recorded similar findings, quoting data of The Audience Agency's Spring 2022 Cultural Participation Monitor, which found that

> 45% of the general population said they had taken part in an online cultural activity during the pandemic. Across nearly all online activities, the same percentages of respondents said they were doing this before the pandemic. Watching a live or recorded performance online is the exception, increasing from 23% to 28%.[43]

Digital theatre appears to reach the younger and more diverse demographics, in addition to the people with disabilities: '45% engagement with online cultural activity is much higher in the 16–24 [age] category and ... those with some specific types of disability were more likely to engage online than the overall average, for example, those who are visually impaired or those with depression or anxiety'.[44] The report concludes that 'this capacity of the digital to engage the young audiences of the future, and its implications in terms of access, mean decisions about the future of their digital offer for regional theatres will be well-considered'.[45] The report also notes some challenges: while audiences agree that 'digital theatre offers convenience and has the capacity to engage remote audiences and overcome geographic barriers, and to provide strategies of access for D/deaf and disabled audiences', many 'find it lacks the "eventness" and thrill of live performance'.[46]

### European Union

In May 2023, the European Theatre Convention, in collaboration with the Academy for Theatre and Digitality in Dortmund, published a study, *Digital Theatre – Strategies and Business Models in European Theatre*, which compiled quantitative and qualitative data for the years 2019, 2020, and 2021 for 19 theatres from 17 European countries. The study measured the impact of the COVID-19 pandemic on the development and role of digital theatre in Europe.[47] In 2020, 26.4 per cent of all tickets sold were for some form of digital theatre (streamed shows and shows made for hybrid and digital spaces), and in 2021, it was 30.9 per cent, with 135,000 tickets sold for digital theatre in both 2020 and 2021.[48] While in-person ticket sales in 2020 dropped to 33.6 per cent of the previous year, and to 28.4 per cent in the year 2021, by comparison, digital theatre grew by 772 per cent between 2019 and 2020, and remained stable throughout 2021.

At the same time, between 2019 and 2021, theatre employment positions specific to digital theatre increased by 263 per cent. Supporting these findings, roles with digital remits in staff increased in European theatres by 268 per cent during the same period. The proportion of freelance or short-term contracted staff with digital roles also increased, from 42.42 per cent in 2019 to 63.7 per cent in 2020. Looking forward, the study offered clues on the potential future of digital theatre, noting that it 'remains divisive'. Of theatres that did not produce any digital content, 74.3 per cent attributed this choice to a 'lack of interest' from their creative team. The study adds that 'it is clear that such theatres hold strong opinions about digital theatre, and many believe it to be in direct opposition to their definition of theatre-making'.[49]

In addition, the report found that European theatres believe the cost of producing digital theatre to be 'challenging or prohibitive', and are concerned 'that digital distribution could replace opportunities for international touring'.[50] However, this is balanced against the clear interest in digital theatre from theatres that did engage in the artform: 83 per cent of theatres that created 'digitally located theatre' reported that it had reached new audiences, and 74% of theatres that used 'digitally mediated theatre' said that it had been a success in terms of creative expression.[51]

The primary barriers to digitalization include financial and infrastructure limitations and complex copyright laws, but also mistaken perceptions about the potential long-term benefits of digitalization on theatre's artistic output and reach. The report underscores the disconnect between audience interest in digital offerings and the perception of that interest by theatres. Although 83 per cent of theatres reported that their digital productions reached 'new audiences', only 36.8 per cent of theatres '"agree or strongly agree" that digital theatre is important to their long-term strategy, while 31.5% of surveyed theatres "neither agree nor disagree" over the importance of digital theatre to long-term strategy'.[52] The report concludes that

> there is often a striking difference between perceptions of low audience interest and reports of high audience

enjoyment, and the development of new audiences. Theatres have raised concerns of 'screen fatigue' in their audiences, but the increased ticket sales for digital theatre in 2021, despite there being fewer productions than in 2020, could suggest that audience interest is in fact rising.[53]

### Australia

In August 2022, Creative Australia released the *National Arts Participation Survey* for the previous years, which included the data on digital arts engagement.[54] The survey's results clearly indicate that

> Australians are increasingly engaging with digital technology to connect, share, create and engage with arts and creativity. In 2022, most Australians engaged with the arts online or through digital platforms (88% up from 82% in 2019). Almost three quarters of Australians, or 71% of the population aged 15 and over, use digital platforms to access creative experiences and art or to create art. Seven in ten Australians use digital platforms to specifically engage with creativity, culture and art (69%), with more than half of Australians using social media platforms to engage with the arts (54%).[55]

The survey notes that the COVID-19 pandemic accelerated online engagement with the arts, while also fuelling artistic experimentation. As in other regions, in Australia too, younger respondents were more inclined to use digital platforms for creating and consuming arts:

> Almost one third of Australians use digital platforms to create art (31%). Young Australians are the most likely to use digital platforms to create art (62% of those aged 15–24 compared to 38% of those aged 25–49 and 13%

> of those aged 50 and over), most notably to create videos (29% of those aged 15–24 compared to 13% of those aged 25–49 and 2% of those aged 50 and over).[56]

Overall, the comparative analysis of these artistic frameworks in four distinct regulatory and funding models reveals similar trends towards increased digital engagement with performing arts accelerated by the pandemic. Younger and more diverse audiences in particular have embraced digital programming, but older audiences also found the ease of digital access beneficial. Although the trend subsided after the lockdowns were lifted, many audience members continued to access performing arts via digital platforms, despite the significant reduction of digital offerings by the performing arts organizations.

## Performing arts after the pandemic

In 2020, Kwame Kwei-Armah, then artistic director of The Young Vic in the UK, boldly pronounced that 'the cost of filming shows for streaming online will need to be hardwired into budgets post COVID-19'. Theatre, he argued, has been operating 'in the 20th century until now'. Kwei-Armah made the comments during a panel on the digital future of the performing arts at the CogX Global Leadership Summit and Festival of AI:

> After this lockdown there will not be a theatre board that will not sanction some kind of capture of the majority of the shows that a theatre produces. I think we've learned that lesson – that we were in the 20th century. It's going to need to be hard-wired into the budget that shows are captured and then possibly streamed, depending on one's relationship to the audience.[57]

Kwei-Armah further added that it would be 'backwards' to disregard the importance of digital accessibility for excluded audiences: 'we believe in access for all, and to ignore technology and its power to give accessibility to a space would be rather backwards thinking'.[58] In March 2020, Tarek Iskander, the artistic director of Battersea Arts Centre, wrote in similar spirit in the article published in *The Stage*, 'Let's not squander this once-in-a-generation opportunity. Let's think long-term and think big.'[59]

Unfortunately, neither one of these calls has been heard, as most theatres in the UK and around the world promptly shut down their streaming ventures once audiences were allowed to return to in-person venues. 'During Covid lockdowns, there was much talk about the need for theatre to change. A return to normal was not an option', wrote Alistair Smith, the researcher and editor at *The Stage*, in February 2024: 'The damage inflicted by Covid, coupled with a worsening economic situation, meant many of these good intentions never came to fruition. Instead, theatre leaders were so desperate to welcome back audiences that, by and large, things went back to how they always were.'[60] How were things for people with disabilities and marginalized audience members (and theatre-makers)?

Commissioned in 2021 by the British Council (within the context of Europe Beyond Access, the world's largest transnational Arts & Disability project), the 'Time to Act' report, the first-ever transnational study of performing arts artists and audiences with disabilities across 42 countries, notes that

> 48% of respondents were not very confident or not at all confident in the accessibility of artistic programmes for disabled artists. The report shows greater engagement around access for disabled audiences, with a lower figure of 39% not very confident or not at all confident in the accessibility of artistic programmes for disabled audiences.[61]

The report points out that while people with disabilities are eager to participate in cultural offerings, they are precluded from doing so by 'physical access, health issues, economic aspects, distance to venues, personal isolation and problems with online booking of events'.[62] The 'Time to Act' report concludes that

> While the last 18 months have increased online and remote working, and seen a broader turn towards digital approaches that may provide a path to greater access, participants in Time to Act's research repeatedly raised concerns that ongoing health risks impact disabled people disproportionately, that tighter resources could push inclusion strategies off the agenda for funders and others in the cultural field, and that disabled people 'will disappear once again from the public space'.[63]

These fears have been justified and mostly realized. By 2022, once the COVID-19 restrictions had been lifted, most theatres in the US, as well as in the UK, the EU, and Australia, returned to their previous in-person programming, abandoning their streaming modalities and infrastructure and the disabled audiences they served. Likewise, the online and hybrid performing arts experiments that took place during the early months of the pandemic were also mostly curtailed and often abandoned.

The 2024 Exeter University report notes that the financial expectations for digital offerings (to either break even or to generate sustainable income) conflicted with those for in-person programming (assumed to require subsidies from state or private sources). This discrepancy in perceptions of financial outcomes contributed to eventual reduction and closure of digital programmes. After the lockdowns,

> the organisations struggled to maintain their digital offer while re-starting in person, with some offering live-digital programme hybrids, maximising accessibility by catering for the majority of D/Deaf and disabled arts

> participants who remained interested in the digital offer. ... However, the expectation that digital programmes should break even makes it hard to compete with subsidised in-person provision, which risks excluding a considerable portion of the population.[64]

The return to pre-pandemic in-person programming, however, did not provide the much-sought-after financial stability, as theatres across all four regions have been grappling with lower audience attendance, funding cuts, and post-pandemic economic challenges.

### United Kingdom

In the UK, the DAAC report noted a significant decrease of online streaming following the loosening of COVID-19 restrictions:

> In the first 18 months of the pandemic of the 219 publicly funded theatres and theatre companies in the UK, 123 (56%) streamed live performances, offered digitally native performances, or offered online workshops. For the autumn 2021 season, this figure went down to 60 (28%), and in the winter/spring 2022 season, this figure went down again to 35 (16%). In autumn 2021, 68% of touring companies that had previously offered streaming content were no longer doing so; for receiving houses the figure was 45% and for producing theatres 49%. In winter/spring 2022, 82% of touring companies that had that had previously offered streaming content were no longer doing so; for receiving houses the figure was 55% and for producing theatres 76%.[65]

The post-pandemic recovery of in-person programming for UK theatres presents a complex and conflicting picture of the performing arts landscape. In 2024, the Indigo Ltd. report,

'Tomorrow's Audiences', noted that 'the first-time theatregoers made up 54% of all ticket bookers' in 2023, with new audiences being younger and more diverse.[66] At the same time, the 'Theatres Beyond the Stage' 2022 report noted that while most audiences returned to in-person programming, there is a sizeable 'lost audience' in the UK theatre ecosystem.[67] In 2025, *The Stage* wrote about a report from Society of London Theatre and UK Theatre, 'which predicts that a third of theatres will run at a deficit this financial year'. Regional theatres in particular were at risk of bankruptcy.[68]

In general, due to funding cuts in government subsidies and to the inflation that shrank disposable incomes, UK theatres have been slow to recover their in-person programming, while neither maintaining nor expanding their digital offerings. Kwei-Armah himself, discouraged by the funding cuts and reluctant audiences, stepped down from his position as artistic director in 2024.[69] *The Stage* critic Amanda Parker commented this way on his departure:

> Kwei-Armah's departure highlights much about how we work. It sheds harsh light on sector-wide planning and its capacity to pivot in the face of what is now a well-worn litany of challenges: the pandemic's impact on theatre, the rising cost of living, the unpredictability of box office as advance bookings dwindle.[70]

In 2023, *The Guardian* reported that Kwei-Armah was not the only artistic director to quit his job. Challenged by reduced funding, 'burnout and disillusionment', UK artistic directors of small and mid-sized regional UK theatres have been quitting 'in droves'.[71] Likewise, the theatre programmes at UK universities have faced draconian budget cuts, forcing them to navigate a 'funding model that is widely acknowledged to be unfit for purpose'.[72] The combination of funding reductions, economic challenges, and the ongoing impact of COVID-19 on theatre-going communities has compelled some theatres to reckon with their audience engagement and analogue-only programming. Few, however, have considered broadening their digital offerings as part of a long-term solution.[73]

The apparent lack of interest in accommodating marginalized populations seems to have also contributed to low optimism among theatre-makers with disabilities. A 2023 Creative Access report reveals that while 59 per cent of theatre professionals express optimism about their career futures, disabled individuals across various creative industries, including theatre, reported the lowest levels of career optimism. Only 30 per cent of respondents with disabilities felt optimistic about their future career prospects – a stark 13 per cent decline since Creative Access conducted similar research in 2022.[74]

In March 2025, Indigo Ltd published a survey report, 'Access Culture', which noted that over half of disabled audiences (52 per cent) reported missing cultural events because venues lacked appropriate seating options. Additionally, 38 per cent of individuals with disabilities have avoided events because they weren't confident their accessibility needs would be met. These challenges stand in stark contrast to the experience of nondisabled attendees, of whom only 3 per cent reported being unable to attend events for similar reasons.[75] At the same time, '71% of disabled visitors struggle to find key venue information, with unclear websites and missing details creating barriers'.[76] The report found that 'uncertainty, lack of confidence in accessibility, and feeling unwelcome also deter attendance'.[77] Issues such as physical barriers, staff and public attitudes, and sensory overloads add to the barriers for in-person access. The report underscores the difficulties faced by the audience members with disabilities in accessing live events in person, and further indicates the need to both improve in-person access and boost digital access. In the context of broader accessibility needs, digital accessibility is just one component of an ongoing accessibility issues.

In 2025, Boston Consulting Group's (BCG) Centre for Growth released a report, 'The Next Act: A Vision for the UK's Creative Future', which assessed that 'Streaming services, skills shortages, and the rise of artificial intelligence are causing the UK's creative industries to lag behind their global competitors'. To stay ahead, UK cultural sector should attempt to 'stream its content to wider audiences and provide more technical courses for younger students'.[78] Surprisingly, in 2025, a Society of London Theatre and UK Theatre organized an online event focused on 'future-proofing theatre for next generations'. The panel featured director Suba Das, Theatre Royal Wakefield boss Katie Town, and Claire Hodgson, artistic director of Diverse City. One of the proposals included suggestion to use digital 'avatars' for performers, with one of the goals being outreach to 'audiences unable to travel'. 'AI could help the industry make strides forward in terms of accessibility and cost-cutting', *The Stage* reported.[79] This solution, which bypasses the performers, does indicate the new copyright challenges brought by the rise of AI, and its impact on digital accessibility, and indicates the need for theatre artists to get ahead of the issue.

### European Union

The severe impact of the COVID-19 pandemic on theatres is well-documented in Europe. An initial 2021 report by Ernst & Young on the state of the cultural and creative industries in Europe predicted that total revenue in the performing arts would fall by 90 per cent during the year 2020.[80] The 2022 European Commission's study, 'The Situation of Theatres in the EU Member States', added more direct figures.[81] In certain European countries, box office receipts declined by more than 60 per cent: 62 per cent in Lithuania and a staggering 78.45 per cent in Italy. Berlin's publicly funded theatres, orchestras, and dance groups reported a 73 per cent drop in audience numbers. Responding to the shrinking of in-person audiences, by March 2021, 142 national support measures were implemented in 27 EU Member States that could have potentially benefited theatres and the wider Creative and Cultural Sector (CCS). Of these, 15 per cent were theatre-specific.[82] However, finding reliable data for theatres throughout Europe remains challenging, given the sector's diversity and disparity, coupled with the lack of harmonized data at national or EU levels.

The European Commission's study notes that COVID-19 'further accelerated the digital shift in the sector', adding that many European theatres 'were forced to move their activities online in order to maintain their presence and continue their social mission to provide cultural content to society'.[83] The study adds, however, that for many professionals engaged in such activities, this digital work did not provide sufficient income to make up for the jobs they had lost due to limitations imposed on live performances during the acute phase of the pandemic.[84] The artists involved in digital projects 'often work for free – further increasing their precarity'.[85] In addition to these difficulties, or perhaps because of them, the pandemic had 'advanced the exploration of issues relating to copyright, privacy', and other challenges to access within the sector.[86]

In 2022 the European Theatre Convention (ETC) published a study by the Prospero – Extended Theatre project, which is funded by the European Union. Titled *Performing Arts Recordings and Broadcasts – A Practical Manual on Author's and Related Rights*, the study was authored by copyright experts Maxime de Brogniez and Antoine Vandenbulke from the University of Liège and the University of Mons, respectively. It identifies various legal issues that arise across Europe when recording performances and broadcasting them online, alongside practical advice for addressing these concerns.[87] Overall, the study identifies the scale of the challenges, noting that 'a lack of authorization or an inappropriate authorization of the specificities of a recording and an online broadcast can purely and simply block the whole enterprise', with the biggest issues being due to stakeholders 'not receiving complete information'.[88]

### *United States*

In the US, the 'return to normal' has not brought in the audiences in the numbers expected by the performing arts organizations. COVID-19 has not only contributed to the already pre-existing challenges but added new ones. Audiences have been reluctant to attend crowded theatre houses, expecting the streaming to continue. The reliable older theatregoers, who used to make up the bulk of American theatres' subscription base, have not returned to in-person programming in pre-pandemic numbers. Due to a lack of COVID-19 mitigations in public spaces, and the ongoing vulnerability of this age group to COVID complications, 'more than half of older adults still spend more time at home and less time socializing in public spaces than they did pre-pandemic'.[89] As a result, most Broadway, off-Broadway, and regional theatres have been struggling.

In August 2022, the *New York Times* reported that despite star-studded Broadway shows, theatres are not able to keep them going:

> Fewer than half as many people saw a Broadway show during the season that recently ended than did so during the last full season before the coronavirus pandemic. In 2022, the Met Opera saw its paid attendance fall to 61 percent of capacity, down from 75 percent before the pandemic. Many regional theaters reported their ticket sales went down significantly.[90]

Many fear the losses will continue, as audiences' habits changed due to the pandemic, accelerating existing pre-pandemic trends: ageing audiences, decline of subscription models, and lower ticket sales. Not being able to attract younger, more diverse audiences, and with their traditional older patrons still wary of public places, theatres have been limiting the engagements and audience capacity, curtailing their seasons, and laying off their employees in an effort to maintain their overall operations.

For Broadway theatres alone, *Forbes* reported in October 2022, 'Gross income on ticket sales declined from 33 million per week in May to 20 million in September'.[91] 'How can Broadway rebound from COVID-19 and bring audiences back to the theater?', *Tufts Daily* asked, noting that 'One of the biggest fundamental problems with Broadway is that it's not accessible to the general public. Theater fans have to travel to New York and pay hundreds of dollars to see some of the most in-demand shows'.[92] In March and April of 2024, the *New York Times* reported that with the exception of a few successful recent off-Broadway commercial shows,[93] attendance for Broadway shows continues to be down compared with pre-pandemic levels:

> about 17 percent: 9.3 million seats have been filled in the [2023–24] season as of March 3, down from 11.1 million at the same point in 2020. Box office grosses are down, too: Broadway shows have grossed $1.2 billion so far this season, 14 percent below the level in early March of 2020.[94]

In 2022, *Marketplace* reported that the situation is very much similar for regional theatres.[95] The *LA Times* wrote in May 2022 that 'Both operating capacity and audience attendance are down to almost 50% of pre-pandemic levels, and ticket revenue is about one-third of what it was before COVID-19 struck. Artistic directors say this is not sustainable'.[96] In 2023 two large regional US theatres, Center Theatre Group (CTG) in Los Angeles and Oregon Shakespeare Festival (OSF) in Oregon, reported significant financial losses. In June CTG announced layoffs, cutting '10% of its full-time staff as a result of the funding crisis. CTG's managing director and CEO, Meghan Pressman, told the *Times* that the organization's budget deficit is in the millions of dollars'.[97] CTG also halted most of its programming for the 2023–24 season, calling the crisis 'unlike any other in our 56-year history'.[98] Similarly, starting 'in March 2020, as worries about the pandemic were becoming clear in Southern Oregon, OSF laid off about 80% of its workforce'.[99] With plummeting ticket sales, OSF has continued layoffs and budget cuts.

Even the best well-known and best-funded New York theatres have not been spared. In June 2023, the Brooklyn Academy of Music laid off 13 per cent of its staff and limited its season in order to address the 'sizable structural deficit' the organization was forced to address in light of post-pandemic challenges.[100] In July 2023, the leading and most prestigious American nonprofit theatre, the Public, laid off 19 per cent of its staff. Like many other theatres, the Public 'is suffering from the combined effects of falling revenue and rising costs', reported the *New York Times*.[101]

In 2025, Broadway League released a report, 'The Demographics of the Broadway Audience 2023–2024'. According to the report, while the average age of theatregoers rose to 42 in 2023–24, matching 2018–19 levels, and signifying the return of elder audiences back to theatre, the attendance among those 50 and older grew 12 per cent, still remaining 20 per cent below pre-pandemic numbers. Overall, the 2023–24 season had 12.29 million audience members, which is 16.8 per cent below the record-breaking 2018–19 season (last complete season before shutdown). In addition to drop in the attendance of over 50, suburban attendance dropped to 13 per cent of total audience, the lowest in 30 years.[102]

In 2025, The Alliance of Resident Theatres/New York released a report on the post-pandemic audience attendance for nonprofit theatre, noting that it was down 11 per cent the year from 2022 to 2023, while corporate giving was down 80 per cent.[103] These numbers indicate a shrinking sector, and schools started to respond to that fact. Also in 2025, the Brown University/Trinity Rep Master of Fine Arts Programs in Acting and Directing paused indefinitely its new student admissions, 'following analysis and discussion among Brown and Trinity leaders, as well as an external expert review'.[104] Curt Columbus, the artistic director of Trinity Rep and the interim head of the MFA programme stated that the closure of the programme was prompted by the changes in the theatre industry after COVID, mainly, the declining audiences that made the job in theatre increasingly precarious. 'Audiences have not returned in the way that they were before the pandemic', Columbus said. 'It's irresponsible to have students moving through a program that is trying to imagine what its foundational principles are'.[105]

While theatres have struggled to fill in seats for their in-person offerings, in April 2023 the *New York Times* published an article about the impact that decline of their digital programming had on the disabled community: 'When shuttered venues embraced streaming during the pandemic, the arts became more accessible. With live performance back, and streams dwindling, many feel forgotten.'[106] While in-person audiences dwindle, ticket sales plummet, and financial crises intensify, American theatres continue to retreat from the digital streaming advances made during the pandemic, inadvertently leaving behind the marginalized audiences that benefited from the pandemic-era digital access. Despite the inability to attract in-person audiences at the sustainable level, most US theatres are not considering expanding their digital programming, judging the pandemic-related digital outreach to be predominantly a failure.

Few voices in the theatre community commented on the new status quo. 'No one misses the early days and dark theaters of the Covid pandemic', wrote *New York Times* critic Jesse Green in February 2024, 'but the emergency workaround of streaming content was good for a few things anyway. People who formerly could not afford admission suddenly could, since much of it was free, and artists from anywhere could now be seen everywhere, with just a Wi-Fi connection'.[107] In June 2024, Sarah Ruhl published an article in *American Theatre* exalting in-person theatre's communal spirit as a cure for

American loneliness.[108] Yet, whether consciously or not, Ruhl overlooked the fact that the loneliest are those who cannot go to the theatre at all, or sometimes cannot go anywhere. An assumption of theatre's curative function that relies solely on its analogue liveness excludes all those who, for myriad reasons, cannot participate.

### Australia

On 26 August 2020, the House of Representatives Standing Committee on Communications and the Arts began an inquiry into Australia's creative and cultural industries and institutions. The resulting report, 'Sculpting a National Cultural Plan: Igniting a Post-COVID Economy for the Arts', covered three areas: (1) employment, (2) artists' lived experiences of the pandemic, and (3) commonwealth support.[109] As an industry-focused inquiry, submissions came from peak bodies, academics, and artists, rather than audiences/users. The Report and the other sector and government materials – cover barriers to artists with disabilities and the existing supports for them – financial measures, policy initiatives, and training in digital technologies and PPE use, and so on – but take a more generalized approach to consumers of their work and confine issues to the production perspective, rather than consumption.

Part 2, 'Artists' lived experiences of the pandemic', presents the results of an online survey of artists, which received 4,871 responses. Key issues raised in the survey included employment; artistic engagement; health and well-being; financial stress and government support; and digital pivoting. Inquiry participants highlighted the non-economic benefits of the creative and cultural industries, whether in their own right, for their effects on other non-economic benefits, or as contributors to the economy.[110] For example: FASTLab Research Centre (submission 237) cited a survey by QUT of creative-industries business owners and self-employed creatives, which showed that the negative impacts of the pandemic affected 'people with intellectual disability (39 per cent)'.[111]

The report has a section on equity of access with summaries of key issues raised in submissions from organizations that represent people with disabilities. Diversity Arts noted some benefits and challenges in moving to online events:

> Diversity Arts has moved our launches, talks and events online, as have many of our partners, and many people living in regional or remote places and artists living with disability have reported that digital access has led to greater access for them (online attendance, captioning, sign language interpreters). However, there are a range of limitations for organisations and audiences to access including hardware and software costs, online subscriptions (webinars, services such as Zoom), reliable internet, technical support, and the need to invest in new ways to engage with audiences.[112]

Create NSW found that groups varied in the extent of their desire to engage digitally with the arts:

> This included people with disability (71 per cent), caregivers to older adults (66 per cent) and parents of children aged under six (68 per cent). Further, 45 per cent of people with disability were found to be more likely to want an option to attend performances either in-person or watch a livestream. This was compared with an average of 36 per cent for all respondents. Create NSW suggests this confirms 'the role for digital in expanding access to the arts.'[113]

The report's equity of access section concludes by identifying barriers to digital access, including mental health problems, and actions to address them, such as the federal government's Support Act initiatives.

Despite the ambitious pronouncements of the report, however, digital access to performing arts in Australia was quickly curtailed or eliminated altogether once the theatre houses opened. For many disabled Australians, pandemic accessibility was a revelation, and they were disheartened at the sudden exclusion. A 2022 article in the *Guardian* reported some of their responses: 'Live streams through the pandemic were a revelation for disabled and at-risk audiences. Now they're being switched off – and it's a devastating loss.' As one person put it: 'I didn't know what accessibility really meant until the pandemic hit, even though I've been disabled since 2005. … Putting off the panic about how to do life afterwards was part of a night out – it had never occurred to me that things could be different.' Another voice noted:

> I'd had no idea that 'accessible' and 'inclusive' could extend to my body, which doesn't always process competing stimulation kindly. … The more I could participate in the arts without the pain and fatigue of travel – and of countless unamenable elements out of my control – the more I realised: the online option was a total revelation.[114]

The article concludes:

> Remotely streamed events are a glittering pot of gold not just for disabled people or those vulnerable to Covid infection, but also for regional and national audiences, and parents of young children. … The arts are celebrating going back to normal – live events are back on; streaming is being turned off – but for many of us it's as though the industry has their fingers in their ears and their backs turned on those who aren't safe to participate. It's infuriating and painful to watch. With Covid a mass disabling event, surely access should be kept as a priority? Why waste all that wisdom, time and money? We've

> learned that being included from home is possible. Out of sight, out of mind isn't good enough anymore.[115]

In November 2023, Creative Australia released a report on 'the use of digital media in theatre and how and why audiences are choosing to engage, or not engage, with these innovations'.[116] The report noted an increase engagement with online theatre, particularly among younger audiences. More than half of 'theatregoers attended performances both in-person and online in the preceding 12 months (53%) and 44% attended in-person only'.[117] Australian online audiences consider digital theatre 'convenient, accessible and affordable'.[118] Despite these findings, in Australia too, the theatres scaled back their digital offerings post-pandemic.

The COVID-19 lockdowns prompted a digital pivot in the performing arts, yielding numerous accessibility benefits to previously excluded audiences. Data from the US, the UK, European Union, and Australia reveal similar trends during and after the pandemic: enhanced digital programming boosted participation among disabled, elderly, and younger, more diverse audiences. However, for various reasons, the majority of theatres across the four regions chose to limit or eliminate their digital offerings.

# THREE

# Successful Case Studies

Outreach and engagement can expand access to performing arts and include audiences previously and currently marginalized whether due to geographic location, economics, disability, or medical vulnerability. Although most of these experiments initiated during the lockdowns were financially ineffective, some did succeed. What made some theatre companies successful during the pandemic pivot towards digital streaming? What technological, aesthetic, and dramaturgical strategies were employed by these theatre companies to grow their audiences and increase their earning potential? Answering these questions is essential for the development of a more equitable, accessible, and sustainable model of performing arts culture.

The 2024 report by the Societies and Cultures Institute at Exeter University on 'Pandemic Preparedness in the Live Performing Arts' noted that pre-existing experience with digital tools as well as broad networks of collaborators from diverse professional backgrounds contributed to the success of the companies:

> Prior experience of digital production and existing digital infrastructure, skills and resources, along with strong existing partnerships and relationships with non-cultural partners or significant experience of community engagement contributed to organisations' resilience. Where these strengths and partnerships were in place, organisations found themselves more easily able to pivot into digital activity or engage in work that sustained or

> built on local presence and contributed to maintaining staff skills and morale. Adaptability was not always linked to size, since some smaller organisations found themselves able to flex more easily, and some larger ones benefitted from significant existing investments. … Those whose existing business models were not dependent on a building were quicker to pivot.[1]

Here are some examples of larger and smaller theatre companies and organizations that were able to pivot successfully to digital programming albeit with some private and public subsidies.

## United States

In January 2023, tech and theatre entrepreneurs Jim Augustine and Oren Michels co-founded the all-new League of Live Stream Theater (LOLST), a nonprofit organization aiming to make Broadway and regional theatre productions available via streaming.[2] LOLST bills itself as 'a nonprofit that provides technical and financial solutions nonprofit theatres need to efficiently deliver their content to a global audience'.[3] Augustine and Michels, both passionate about supporting the theatre industry, initially crossed paths during the pandemic while negotiating a deal to livestream Second Stage's production of Lynn Nottage's *Clyde's*. Augustine, then working for Zuckerberg Media and Assemble Stream Inc., had developed the necessary infrastructure for the project, while Michels, a Second Stage board member, aimed to broaden the organization's reach. *Clyde's* became the first Broadway show to be simulcast, demonstrating the potential for live theatre to reach worldwide audiences while generating substantial revenue and attracting new viewers to Second Stage. For *Clyde's*, tickets were priced at $59 per household, and 120 per cent of the initially allotted inventory was sold, with 90 per cent at full price. The livestream reached a significant audience, nearly double the capacity of the physical theatre.

Supported by Bloomberg Philanthropies, LOLST aimed to make theatre more accessible worldwide by streaming live performances to homes, schools, community centres, and other underprivileged communities. Since its launch, and through partnerships with various theatre organizations, LOLST successfully livestreamed productions such as *Between Riverside and Crazy*, *Miscast 2023*, *Endgame*, and *The Children*. They managed to do so by significantly reducing production costs below the traditional theatre filming services. LOLST's strategy involved offering time-limited livestreams and cultivating a shared list of interested audience members among partner institutions. The majority of their audience falls between the ages of 55 and 74, with viewers in NYC tending to buy tickets to more shows than regional viewers. The organization has identified common barriers to attending live theatre, such as chronic illness, mobility issues, visual obstructions, ticket prices, crowd discomfort, and auditory challenges.

LOLST achieved marketing success through targeted direct marketing, earned media placements, and cross-promotional partnerships with member theatres. As LOLST grows, it faces challenges such as addressing accessibility concerns, navigating rights issues with theatre-makers, and establishing trust with unions. The organization is actively exploring new avenues for growth, including residencies, partnerships, advanced production grants, data-driven union relations, and public–private collaborations. Additionally, LOLST is considering partnering with publishers of major play anthologies to integrate lower-resolution videos into educational curricula, facilitating the use of both text and video content in classroom settings.[4]

The second successful American case study worth highlighting involves a small Massachusetts-based theatre company, ARLEKIN! Unlike most other performing arts institutions, who saw their audiences and their budgets collapse during the COVID lockdowns, ARLEKIN! expanded their audiences thanks to their innovative digital interactive strategies, reaching previously hidden national and international demographics. ARLEKIN! grew from a small, regional theatre in MA into an international phenomenon selling thousands of tickets thanks to its digital and hybrid programming model.

When the pandemic forced theatre closures worldwide, ARLEKIN! quickly pivoted and leaned into the innovative possibilities of virtual-theatre productions. The company combined multiple technologies – animation, gaming, and virtual environments – to create a completely new experience that the *New York Times* called 'ingenious'.[5] With the reopening of theatres, ARLEKIN!'s experimentation continued to make hybrid productions that create uniquely different experiences for virtual and in-person audiences who are seeing the same live performance together.

Within two months of lockdowns, the company premiered *State vs Natasha Banina*: a free, live, Zoom-cast, virtual-theatre event which toured virtually around the world through local international presenting venues. ARLEKIN! began to successfully leverage dozens of interested international partners to present and further develop its work. This launched ARLEKIN!'s virtual-theatre initiative, Zero Gravity (zero-G) Lab, which has since produced two more new virtual-theatre pieces: *chekhovOS/an experimental game/*, with a cast led by the legendary Mikhail Baryshnikov and celebrated TV/Broadway actress Jessica Hecht (*Friends*, *Breaking Bad*), and *Witness*, a world-premiere documentary developed with researchers at the US Memorial Holocaust Museum, which drew audiences from 55 countries.

Building on its success, ARLEKIN! next developed a critically celebrated off-Broadway production of *The Orchard*, a new adaptation of *The Cherry Orchard*, featuring both Baryshnikov and Hecht and the talents of an international design team (US, Brazil, Ukraine, Poland). It combined animation, robotics, gaming, and other technologies to form a hybrid in-person and virtual production that ran for 31 performances at the Baryshnikov Arts Center in New York

City in June–July 2022 and a second run, hosted at Emerson's Paramount Theatre in Boston, in November 2022.

ARLEKIN!'s virtual programming reached previously neglected audiences. Building on its ethos of inclusion, ARLEKIN!'s Boston production of *The Orchard* featured Seth Gore, a Deaf bilingual actor and DASL (Director of American Sign Language), specializing in interplay between English and ASL languages, arts, teaching, and technology. The New York production featured Deaf actor John McGinty. The characters they played communicated using American Sign Language during the performances. Additionally, Google captioning was used by patrons during virtual performances. In 2023, the company staged the hybrid (in-person and virtual) version of *The Gaaga*, written and directed by Sasha Denisova, with the virtual piece directed by Igor Golyak. Like other shows, *The Gaaga* was live, interactive, and hybrid.

By seamlessly incorporating digital technology in its in-person, hybrid, and virtual productions, ARLEKIN! was able to develop an organic, universal model of inclusivity that appealed to both traditional theatre-going audiences and younger digital natives, as well as many formerly excluded and marginalized communities, including the people with disabilities, the elderly, geographically distant, and economically disadvantaged. During each project, ARLEKIN! sought ways to help the audience interact with the artistic product. This was accomplished through live auctions, live conversations with actors, video streams captured and integrated into the production (allowing the audience to see themselves together), voting, surveys, chats among audience members, shopping, and so on. What the company uncovered was not only a worldwide audience that craved performances during the pandemic, but also an underrepresented community that has benefited from these experiments. People who are homebound, with mobility issues, and those with limited or no hearing and sight were provided access to award-winning, critically acclaimed productions that would otherwise not be available to them.

ARLEKIN! and its zero-G Lab have essentially ridden the wave of a new emerging genre of performance art at the nexus of theatre, film, gaming, animation, and interaction.[6]

## United Kingdom

Large, well-funded UK theatres began launching successful streaming and digital programming even before the pandemic. In 2009, the National Theatre introduced its digital broadcasting programme NT Live. In 2014, Jen Peters wrote about the programme:

> While previous live transmissions of theatre took place on TV or on the internet, *NT Live* with its reach of about 260 cinema screens in the UK and an additional 390 screens in over 25 countries world-wide marks the beginning of the live broadcast as a nation-wide and indeed global large-scale event.[7] Digital broadcast of performances in cinemas had been pioneered by the Metropolitan Opera in New York in 2006, which have been followed by other international arts institutions. Nonetheless, the National Theatre in London was the first *theatre* to attempt the live cinema broadcast of its performances. Since 2009 [until 2013], NT Live has shown 29 productions to a global audience including spectators in the USA, Australia, South Africa, New Zealand, and Germany. The first two experimental broadcasts of NT Live, *Phèdre* and *All's Well That Ends Well,* were made possible by funding from Arts Council England and NESTA (National Endowment for Science, Technology and the Arts). For subsequent broadcasts, the National Theatre was able to attract the sponsorship of insurance company AVIVA. *NT Live* has clearly been a success in terms of audiences, and other theatre companies are following in its footsteps: the Royal Shakespeare Company will broadcast its production of

> *Richard II* 'in more than 100 cinemas, overseas as well as in Britain'.[8,9]

Audiences responded enthusiastically to the digital programming, which further elevated the National Theatre's profile. Peters continues:

> It is not, as many people have feared, a stale and stilted imitation of theatre, but is able to create its own unique viewing experience and atmosphere. Since its beginning, NT Live has attracted 1,5 million people,[10] amongst them a large section of lower income audience, thereby potentially acting as a gateway into theatre.[11] Moreover, performance rights were negotiated openly and fairly, a process that has resulted in benefitting not only the National Theatre, but the artists involved in the creation of the performance.[12] Given this success and the influence NT Live is likely to have on the development of digital broadcasts of theatre in the UK and elsewhere, it is crucial to pose some fundamental questions about the nature and implications of such a mediatisation of theatre alongside the already present acknowledgement of its potentials in promoting theatre.[13]

The National Theatre's pre-pandemic success with digital programming was remarkable. Thanks to its substantial funding and its role as a flagship institution representing British culture internationally, the National Theatre was well positioned to take bold steps. It invested in digital infrastructure and human resources, purchasing the necessary equipment and establishing a dedicated digital dramaturgy department. Since 2014, the National Theatre has continued to expand its digital programming, often setting the benchmark and overshadowing other initiatives in the field. In April 2024, Rufus Norris reflected on the success of NT Live in an article for *The Stage*:

> Over the past 15 years, 100 theatre productions have been broadcast as part of NT Live. And despite initial scepticism, … the project has proved digital theatre access is a force for good – for audiences and the industry.
>
> When the NT Live 'experiment' launched with *Phèdre* starring the magnificent Helen Mirren in 2009 – broadcasting to around 270 venues worldwide – I confess, I was a complete sceptic. I knew that theatre was dependant on the live relationship between audience member and actor, and any compromise was suspect. I had too often seen a terrible archive recording of something made with care shot from the back of the stalls, and withered with shame at the resulting record. I was wrong.
>
> [M]y objection revealed an exclusive snobbery. I live in London, and even before my current position, I could hustle my way into many shows I wanted to see. For the multitudes for which neither were true, NT Live gave a high-quality access to something they could otherwise only read about.
>
> Since then, NT Live has grown exponentially, screened in more than 2,500 venues across 70 countries, and reaches upwards of 11 million people worldwide. I have lost count of the people who have approached me to simply express gratitude that they can see at least some of London's theatre, whether in Budapest or Bridport.[14]

Although the success of NT Live is closely tied to the National Theatre's unique position within the UK's cultural landscape, it nonetheless offered a concrete model that has since been adopted – albeit with less panache – by smaller, less well-funded, yet stable theatre companies. The UK report on 'Digital Access to Arts and Culture (DAAC)' highlights several successful hybrid projects that blend traditional and digital forms.[15] One notable example is *Paradise*, which premiered in 2022 as part of the second season of Darkfield Radio. Created by the immersive theatre company Darkfield, *Paradise* is one of the six audio performances designed for at-home listening. It is described as 'an AI powered immersive audio experience designed for couples, exploring why we stay together or fall apart'.[16] While Darkfield had already staged in-person, 360-degree binaural performances before the pandemic, the two radio seasons expanded access by allowing audiences to experience the shows remotely too, via a dedicated app. Darkfield Radio sold over 25,000 cumulative tickets to its six shows, which also 'featured in over 20 (live and online) film festivals including Sundance, Venice, and Tribeca, and have been sold to international partners in the USA, Australia and Taiwan'.[17] The DAAC report concludes that the app 'has helped Darkfield to access wider international markets, build a strong brand presence, and form various new international cross-sector partnerships'.[18]

Other case studies featured in the DAAC report stress how digital projects facilitate collaborations with disabled artists, and overall help 'diversify the … artist community', as well as the public.[19] For example, for the creation of the Lowry Digital Now! production *Mystery Trip* (2022), Nigel Barrett and Louise Mari worked with disability and welfare rights activist Kerry Underhill and a group of 12 homebound artists and co-creators, plus nine other 'guests' from locations around the word, from Mexico and Norway to China and New Zealand. Featuring live captions and British Sign Language translation, *Mystery Trip* took audiences on globe-trotting virtual journeys.

The DAAC report also uses the example of the Royal Court and Black Ticket Project 2020 co-production of the Zoom show *My White Best Friend (and Other Letters Left Unsaid)* as an opportunity to ask whether streaming video can 'upscal[e] the use of ticket giveaways as a route to greater inclusion'.[20] The performances consisted of Black actors reading letters written by ten Black writers 'that say the unsaid', followed by open discussions with the public in small break-out rooms.[21] The show was ticketed, and demand far exceeded expectations – by a factor of ten, according to the Royal Court – ultimately generating around £18,000 in revenue. Tickets were priced at either £12 or £5, and notably, 80 per cent of spectators chose the higher price. This pricing model enabled the theatre to offer 50 per cent of the available tickets for free through the Black Ticket Project, supporting greater access and inclusivity. Since the Zoom platform imposed a limit on participants, the DAAC investigators wondered how the show could have reached an even greater public via streaming.

## European Union

The 2023 European Theatre Convention (ETC) report presents two case studies showcasing the successful use of digital tools by European theatres between 2019 and 2022.[22] A key feature shared by both case studies is that the theatres began experimenting with hybrid programming even before COVID-19 restrictions curtailed live performance. With the initiative led by Joachim Nordwall, the Folkteatern in Gothenburg, Sweden, added in September 2017 a digital Fourth Stage (Fjärde Scenen) to the physical performance venues they already possessed. Meanwhile, in Kyiv, Andrii Palatnyi, affiliated with Dakh Theatre – Centre of Contemporary Arts and Gogolfest, Ukraine's largest arts festival, worked to mobilize funding partners and assemble technical and human resources. This effort came at a time when digital innovation was not yet a priority in the local theatre arts sector. Even though these initial plans fell through once the pandemic hit, Palatnyi reported to the ETC investigator Katie Hawthorne that the prior interest in digital affordances enabled the Dakh to 'jump in' to developing a digital repertoire that proved crucial for weathering the financially difficult times ahead.[23]

For the Folkteatern, the pandemic intensified activities on the Fourth Stage, as it became the only open stage available to the entirety of the theatre's cast and crew members. Within the short span of four months, the Folkteatern produced 12 filmed theatre works under the umbrella programme 'Urgent Drama'. Despite the significantly increased usage of the digital stage by artists and spectators alike, Nordwall expresses some reservations. He doesn't believe that a digital stage is best used as 'a platform for film', limited to 'documentation of physical performances'.[24] He singles out instead a commissioned work that premiered in 2020, Spanish artist Cha Blasko's *I Breathe*, as a better example of the rich potential that may be unlocked by hybrid projects. *I Breathe* takes place simultaneously online on the Fourth Stage – as an interactive installation that transforms air quality data into sound – and as a live performance in a black box theatre where Blasko plays the installation like an instrument.

For Nordwall, such a hybrid project opens new possibilities for what digital theatre can become. It points to new models for engaging artists in mutually beneficial, longer-term partnerships. In the context where many theatres worry that digitally availability might undercut financially vital touring opportunities, *I Breathe* offers compelling alternative touring models. Each time Blasko performs the piece internationally, the number of visitors to the Fourth Stage installation increases. At the time of the report, the online installation *I Breathe* has accumulated over 10,000 unique views.

One production that emerged out of Gogolfest's experimental laboratory during the 2020 lockdown was *Alone [Digital Odyssey]*, directed by Dakh founder Vlad Troitskyi. In line with social distancing regulations, the hybrid performance relied on digital screens and invited 20 audience members at a time. Palatnyi also speaks of the hybrid programme of the 2021 iStage festival in Mariupol that merged live performances and discussions with screenings and broadcasts to expand the festival's reach both in terms of artistic collaborations and audience engagement within and across borders. The necessity of this vision only intensified once Russia invaded Ukraine in 2022. Dakh Theatre launched an 'Art Resistance Programme' that produced projects such as the audiovisual installation *Alarm* and the musical documentary *Danse Macabre*. The latter uses 'a lot of LED [lights] and loop pedals to create a complicated sound environment'.[25]

Despite the reported artistic and institutional successes of theatres like Folkteatern and Dakh with their forays into the digital – particularly as adaptive responses to social, economic, and political challenges – the ETC report reveals a persistent reluctance among many European theatres to follow their lead. While 13 out of the 19 European theatres surveyed in the ETC study viewed digital theatre as a 'short-term solution' in the context of a global pandemic, only seven considered it as important component of their 'long-term strategy'.[26]

## Streaming platforms

During the last few years, a number of public and private initiatives have emerged that attempt to make recordings of theatre and opera productions available either via open access or via subscription to streaming platforms modelled on Netflix or Hulu. Some examples of open-access portals include OperaVision, 'a free opera streaming platform, supported by the European Union's Creative Europe programme';[27] Ninateka, a Polish platform sponsored by the Polish Ministry of Culture and European Union Fund for Regional Development, which hosts over 7,000 videos of Polish theatre, film, and animation;[28] and Madelen, a platform sponsored by the French government to host a collection of French movies, broadcasts, and theatre shows.[29] Both Madelen and Ninateka are predominantly focused on the archivization of old, classic, historical shows, while OperaVision tries to capture and showcase contemporary offerings.

Another open-access, state-funded initiative is the Prospero – Extended Theatre project,[30] co-funded by the Creative Europe Programme of the European Union in partnership with ten large European theatres, including Schaubühne Berlin, Teatr Powrzechny in Warsaw, and Odéon-Théâtre de l'Europe in

Paris. Each theatre develops new works which are recorded, digitalized, and broadcast free online with subtitles in eight languages.

In addition to these state-sponsored initiatives, many private start-ups attempting to create a viable business model for online theatre emerged. Among them, a few deserve mention. Marquee.tv[31] wants to be 'Netflix for the Arts'. Its theatre collection, however, is mostly limited to Shakespeare offerings from the Royal Shakespeare Company and the Globe. Another subscription-based project is Dramox.tv,[32] which has a collection focused mainly on Eastern and Central European shows. In the US, BroadwayHD[33] is another subscription model with a focus on commercial Broadway shows and includes a mix of older and new productions. One of the more unorthodox projects is Scenesaver.co.uk,[34] a grassroots platform where theatre artists can submit their shows for others to watch for free. Scenesaver operates on at-will donations from their subscriber base.

Two projects that illustrate the varied challenges of capturing, archiving, and showcasing theatre online are DigitalTheatre, based on individual subscriptions,[35] and its educational component, DigitalTheatrePlus (DT+).[36] DT+ operates on a subscription-based model, with educational institutions as its primary users. Launched in 2009 as a consumer service, DT+ expanded its offerings in 2011 to cater to the educational market. The platform provides access to over 500 productions of key texts, mapped to international curricula, along with a wealth of supplementary materials such as interviews, insights, lesson plans, quizzes, and essays. The company is funded by subscription revenue from these institutions and has paid back £3 million to the creative ecosystem to date. DT+ balances between state and private institutions, with 70 per cent of its US subscribers being state-run. The platform prioritizes accessibility, discoverability, and security while offering a rich diversity of content.

One of the main challenges faced by DT+ is the high cost of capturing live theatre performances. This is primarily due to the high fees demanded by unions, particularly in the US, where capturing a performance can cost multiple times more than in the UK. The company is actively lobbying unions to reduce payments to creatives for educational purposes. Additionally, the technical aspects of capturing a performance, including videography and editing, can be costly. Another challenge is securing the necessary rights for distribution. DT+ requires long rights periods (a minimum of three years) to monetize the content effectively, which can be a point of contention with rights holders. DT+ also faces the challenge of developing new audiences for theatre. The company aims to attract younger audiences who are accustomed to consuming content on platforms like YouTube and TikTok. Digital Theatre's mission has always been 'to break down barriers and make world-class theatre accessible to audiences everywhere' and 'to empower teachers and inspire students'. The company also relies on partnerships with theatres, academics, and educational institutions to expand its reach. DT+ is actively working on reducing capture costs and seeking collaborations with digitally capable theatre companies to push the boundaries of what digital theatre can offer.[37]

Another streaming initiative is the International Online Theatre Festival (IOTF),[38] which showcases a diverse range of theatre productions from around the world. Organized by TheTheatreTimes.com, IOTF is an annual (or biennial) event that streams international theatre shows for free, making them accessible to a wide global audience. The festival aims to create an online space that transcends geographical boundaries while also promoting the decolonization of theatre festivals and providing more accessible modes for theatre encounters. IOTF is a proof-of-concept model, which relies on volunteers and the theatre artists willing to share their shows for free for a duration of one day to two weeks of the festival. One of IOTF's greatest strengths is its commitment to representing all continents and showcasing theatre from regions previously underrepresented on international stages.

Despite the challenges posed by language barriers, the festival has successfully shown productions from a wide range of countries and cultures. In its four editions to date, IOTF has presented over 140 shows from 36 countries, spanning six continents. This diverse programming not only exposes audiences to a variety of theatrical styles and perspectives but also fosters cross-cultural understanding and appreciation of diverse theatre traditions. Another significant aspect of IOTF is making expensive Western productions available to global audiences while also introducing less known local artists to wider publics. By streaming these shows online for free, the festival democratizes access to high-quality theatre and provides a platform for lesser-known, talented artists to gain international recognition. Moreover, IOTF has built a network of scholars and artists through its online discussion panels and thematic focus on urgent social issues, further promoting dialogue and collaboration within the global theatre community.

However, IOTF also faces several challenges. Funding is a major concern, as most foundations and state funding aim to promote their national cultures. Funding for international projects that don't privilege any one particular culture is virtually nonexistent. The language barrier is also an issue, as artists who either speak English themselves or can afford to translate their work have access to broader networks and opportunities. This language barrier can hinder the equal representation of world theatre and exclude valuable contributions from non-English-speaking artists. The festival also faces challenges related to the varied quality of video work submitted by artists. Access to expensive technology can create a rift between rich and poor artists, companies, and institutions. The prioritization of digital output also varies among different theatre-makers. Since IOTF is an all-volunteer project, it is neither sustainable nor a viable model to replicate in other contexts. Nonetheless, as a proof-of-concept, IOTF indicates that there is a strong need for transcultural connections between theatre artists and their audiences which the digital sphere can help to nurture and address. The challenge remains how to facilitate that connection despite the many structural barriers to funding and access.[39]

# FOUR

# Real and Perceived Challenges

Copyright issues around accessibility-focused digitalization are complicated by their connection to broader digitalization copyright concerns. The main challenges to digital accessibility in theatre include financial constraints, misperceptions about the copyright laws and about the cost of digitalization that deter many organizations, lack of technical skills and tools to implement and maintain digital infrastructure, and insufficient marketing skills and familiarity with digital environments. A key factor in theatres' reluctance to continue digital programming is the perceived complexity and confusing nature of streaming copyright laws, which require the additional financial investment that comes with complying with the obligations under copyright law (the complexity of the law requires legal counsel, which in itself is expensive, and which many institutions cannot afford). The 2024 Exeter University report notes the many challenges and concerns, including digital and legal literacy:

> Moves to digital generally favoured larger organisations with existing digital skills, resources and infrastructure. Concerns were raised regarding oversaturation of digital content in a market dominated by 'big players' offering high-quality, freely available archive recordings. Smaller players struggled to compete due to their need to charge for access, raising questions about the financial viability of online performances and digital platforms. Additional concerns arose about varying 'digital maturity'

> among companies, the expectation of high-quality digital and hybrid content and 'booking journeys', and intellectual property and practitioner control over outputs and dissemination.[1]

Most theatres lack knowledge and skills with the specific nature of copyright contracts, which are therefore often perceived as confusing, challenging, and even unfair. Per the European Theatre Convention report, one theatre complained that 'rights holders must agree or approve [every] live stream', and another writes that 'it is now a financial liability to produce work for digital distribution', due to contracts and licensing issues, and the only possibility for sustainable distribution is in external deals with TV broadcasters. The same theatre also described how industry-agreed payment rules require 'creative teams to be paid [for streams] almost as if a further live performance had taken place'.[2]

In addition to these many listed real obstacles, there are others that are perceived as such, though not necessarily backed by research. One of the perceived challenges to digitalization of performing arts is the perception of a 'substitution effect' by the leaders of the arts organizations, a belief that offering digital access to their programming will diminish in-person engagement and thus potentially affect their bottom line. American producers, for example, are concerned that digital offerings will cut into ticket sales.[3] Why would audiences bother to go to the theatre if they can access its programming online? The DAAC report calls this perception the '"substitution effect" in which digital activities cannibalise in-person activities'. However, the DAAC report data determined that the 'substitution effect is a myth', finding

> no evidence either of a sector-wide substitution effect or of any specific examples in which digital engagement eroded in-person engagement. In fact, the opposite seems to be true: … survey revealed that positive experiences

> associated with organisations' online offerings made participants overall more likely to engage with the organisation in person.[4]

The recent data analysis indeed suggests that online offering in fact might complement in-person programming. In their study, 'Beyond the "Substitution Effect": The Impact of Digital Experience Quality on Future In-Person and Online Cultural Participation',[5] Adrian Leguina, Kadja Manninen, and Richard Misek, 'drawing on data from the wide-ranging Digital Experience survey carried out by Indigo Ltd. in 2020–21', noted that a substitution effect does not exist and both in-person and online participation are perceived as 'being able to contribute together to a rich cultural life'.

In his 2024 article for *The Stage*, Rufus Norris also wrote about the fears of 'substitution effect', confirming that based on the decade of the National Theatre's own data, the cannibalization of live audience by the digital one does not exist. In fact, it's the opposite, Norris writes:

> Perhaps the most valid concern – around which there still remains a lingering scepticism – is about the impact of digital theatre on live performance. Some understandably fear that digital theatre cannibalises theatre audiences, drawing them away from the physical experience of attending a play. With so many [100] NT productions available in digital formats, we can share first-hand that these fears are, thankfully, unfounded. In fact, our data and independent surveys show there are no negative effects of announcing a cinema release on in-person ticket sales. In fact, there is some evidence that NT Live can increase live theatre audience numbers, while providing welcome box office to arts centres nationwide that provide both. Additionally, there is increasing proof that an NT Live can benefit the sales of the show being broadcast, adding exposure for the production.[6]

In other words, rather than confirming the widespread perception among theatres of a 'substitution effect' between online and in-person performances, this data suggests a 'complementarity effect'.[7] Based on the successful case studies, it appears that additional online offerings might in fact boost the popularity of a show or theatre company.

## Copyright laws

It is a globally accepted rule that authors of dramatic, dramatico-musical, and musical works need to give permission to authorize the public performance of their works by any means or process. When a theatre company gets permission to play a piece in front of a live audience, there is no presumption that this permission includes the permission to have the play recorded and distributed via broadcasting, streaming, or any other form of communication to the public.[8]

Based on Rome Convention, such a principle does not only exist for the authors of the play. It also exists for the actors performing the play. Whereas authors are protected by copyright or author rights, actors are protected by so-called neighbouring rights or related rights. As a legal instrument they are about a century younger than authors' rights and as a result even less known, even by many copyright experts. In nature they are very similar to each other. Rights that need to be taken into account are the actor's right to authorize the fixation of his/her performance,[9] as well as the right to have such fixations be communicated to the public in any way.[10]

And there are no exceptions to this. In the field of copyright and related rights, there are many exceptions and limitation, but these always apply to a work that has already been fixed. They concern the right of reproduction, the right of communication to the public, but never the right of fixation. The only known exception to the right of fixation is the possibility of the press to report on current events by filming them.[11] But even here the exception is limited to short excerpts. It does not allow the recording of a full work. And it surely does not allow the press to impose on the events they are covering to provide them with the recordings.

Most limitations exceptions to copyright and related rights have been introduced to balance the rights of the different rightsholders with the interest of the general public. This by giving the exception to each individual (right to parody and pastiche, the private copy right, and so on) or by giving the exception to institutions of public interest (exceptions for educational purposes, lending right, and so on). They are never given to a specific group of people, except for one.

With the 2013 Marrakesh Treaty to Facilitate Access to Published Works for Persons Who Are Blind, Visually Impaired or Otherwise Print Disabled (Marrakesh Treaty or MVT), adopted by the World Intellectual Property Organization (WIPO), there is one internationally applied exception that has been introduced to balance copyright with the interest of a specific group of people, the blind, visually impaired, or otherwise print disabled.

The Marrakesh VIP Treaty aims to facilitate access to existing published printed works and introduces a standard set of limitations and exceptions to copyright rules in order to permit the reproduction, distribution, and making available of these published works in formats designed to be accessible to VIPs, and to permit exchange of these works across borders by organizations that serve those beneficiaries.

The conditions to make use of the exception are, however, very strict. It can only be invoked by an authorized entity that exploits the accessible copies made in a noncommercial manner that does not conflict with the normal exploitation of the work. Under the exception, an authorized entity would, for instance, be allowed to provide an audiobook version of an existing book without obtaining the permission of the author or their editor. However, when there is already a commercially available audiobook available, it is highly unlikely that an additional version would be accepted under the exception.

It is also important to highlight that the exception offers the possibility to produce an accessible copy. It does not offer the right to demand that such copy to be provided by the author or publisher. Currently the Marrakesh VIP Treaty is the only example of where copyright law and disability rights are balanced against each other, resulting in a set of internationally agreed limitations and exceptions. For the rest, persons with disabilities – whatever the nature of the disability – must try to make do with the general exceptions that exist.

Indeed, more is needed. However, an exception to copyright does not guarantee access. Even abolishing copyright entirely will not automatically result in accessible recorded versions of all the world's plays. Even if we were to apply the Marrakesh VIP Treaty to theatre performances, this would not lead to an obligation for theatre-makers to provide their live performances in a format that is accessible to people who cannot attend the live performance. As a result, when a theatre wants to make an audiovisual fixation of a play and disseminate this to an additional audience via broadcasting or streaming, it will need additional permission from both author(s) and actor(s). This can be done via an individual contract, but in most countries, this is dealt with via collective management organizations or via collective bargaining agreements with unions.

In Europe, copyright and related rights are a matter for which the EU has a harmonizing competence. As a result, the EU has already adopted an extensive series of directives on the matter that, for authors, result in a strong set of rules. The most important ones are the 2001 Infosoc Directive,[12] and more recently the 2019 DSM Directive.[13] The latter imposes that the authors and performers who license or assign their exclusive rights to use their works have the right to an *appropriate and proportional* remuneration at the actual or potential value of the rights that are granted under license or are assigned.[14,15]

For actors however, these instruments are far from providing a similar or harmonized framework. Actors still have the right to authorize the fixation of their performance, but once a performance has been recorded, the possibilities for actors to control the way these recordings are distributed are very limited. The chance of getting remunerated for additional exploitations is almost nonexistent. Several countries have installed certain statutory remuneration mechanisms that guarantee actors to get additional remunerations for broadcasting, retransmissions and – more recently – streaming and downloading. These are rather the exception than the rule. In practice, actors in the EU face buyouts, and the segmentation of the market means that the unions are also segmented and do not have the bargaining power of their US colleagues to get their actors out of lump-sum buyout contracts. It is therefore comprehensible that actors are reluctant to allow their theatre performances to be recorded and distributed via digital platforms.

## Digital accessibility and disability laws

Disability rights laws in the US, the UK, European Union, and Australia are worded differently and ambiguously enough to be subject to interpretation, placing varied degrees of obligation on companies and institutions to provide digital access to their disenfranchised audiences. Similarly, transnational treaties on disability rights are vague enough to allow signatory countries to balance copyright laws against disability laws. As a result, disabled audience members and others unable to participate in analogue events have no legal recourse to request digital formats.

Based on the existing Marrakesh VIP Treaty, one might argue that theatres shouldn't be obliged to provide accessible formats to homebound patrons since publishers aren't legally required to provide books in Braille (though visually impaired readers can make copies or can have their proxies make copies in any format without fear of copyright breach). However, this argument suggests that the financial burden of access should always rest with the disabled person, which is not the case in any of the legal regimes presented here. Wheelchair users aren't required to carry their own ramps or install their own elevators; spaces with public access – theatres, hotels, restaurants – are legally obliged to build them. Thus, there's a misalignment between how disability rights laws treat book publishers (sellers of culture) versus how they treat public spaces, restaurants, hotels, and so on (sellers of other commodities). Theatres – being both public spaces and sellers of culture – seem to exist in a liminal sphere between these two interpretations of the law. This is what makes the interlocking of copyright and disability laws for live performances so challenging.

Furthermore, based on the Marrakesh VIP Treaty, one might argue that making a building physically accessible is fundamentally different from making the 'work' itself accessible. However, this argument implicitly suggests that some forms of accessibility (and by extension, some types of disability) are more deserving of accommodation than others. It creates an artificial hierarchy between physical accessibility needs (space-based needs), such as those of people with mobility impairments (wheelchair ramps and elevators), and content accessibility needs, like those of individuals with visual impairments or individuals who are homebound due to their disabilities. This distinction fails to recognize that truly inclusive access to culture requires addressing all forms of accessibility barriers equally. Whereas theatres and bookstores are legally obliged to provide wheelchair-accessible spaces (as noted, wheelchair users do not have to carry their own ramps or pay for their construction), they are not legally required to provide disability access to the content they create and sell. In the case of books, visually impaired readers are allowed to make accessible copies of the work for themselves without impinging on the copyright of the book author. However, for live shows, disabled audience members who are unable to attend due to their disabilities are neither provided with a digital format nor allowed to create their own accessible formats. This discrepancy highlights the complex interplay between physical accessibility, content accessibility, and copyright law.

Moreover, based on the Marrakesh VIP Treaty, one could also argue that companies are only obliged to provide access to existing services and content (live shows), not to create new fixed content (recording). This is a common interpretation of many accessibility laws and directives. However, a counterargument would posit that the live show itself is the existing content, with the digital format serving merely as an accessible proxy. From this perspective, a digital version isn't new content but rather an alternative format of the same content. Books in Braille aren't considered new content (not classified as derivative works): they are accessible formats of existing content, which is permissible under the copyright law as defined by the Marrakesh VIP Treaty. This reframing challenges the notion that creating a digital version is equivalent to creating new content. Instead, it positions the digital version as an 'accessible proxy' – a means for those unable to attend in person to access the original content. The argument raises important questions about how we define content in various formats. It highlights the complexity of applying traditional accessibility concepts to the performing arts, especially as technology blurs the lines between live and digital experiences.[16]

### United States

Currently, in the US, the Americans with Disabilities Act (ADA) provides specific guidelines for the accessibility of performing arts events, but they are limited to space and architectural accessibility (ramps, wheelchair-accessible routes of travel, accessible bathrooms, and spaces for wheelchair users and their companions), interpreters or surtitles (for deaf and visually impaired audience members), and website accessibility (including accessible ticketing processes). Although the ADA is now over 30 years old, the theatre industry in the US is still very much behind in its implementation, often not able to provide even these basic accommodations. Quoted in *American*

*Theatre* in 2021, disability scholar Jason Dorwart noted that 'access is often an afterthought'.[17] Theatre manager Howard Sherman points out the irony of treating disability access as a footnote: 'there's no reason why theatres can't proactively review and bring themselves into compliance with [ADA]. If equity, diversity, and inclusion are truly goals for the field, accessibility should be as well. And not just because it's the law'.[18]

The ADA itself, *American Theatre* points out, has too many loopholes allowing 'businesses to neglect accessibility if such efforts constitute an "undue hardship." Many also feel the act has too malleable a definition of what a "reasonable accommodation" is', allowing theatres to evade compliance.[19] In 2010, the United States Department of Justice (DOJ) published revised ADA Standards for Accessible Design, updating the original 1991 Standards. Designated as 'Places of Public Accommodation', theatres fall under ADA Title III, 28 CFR, Part 36. In some ways, the updated Standards increased access (by providing for more equitable ticketing systems), but in others, they limit it (by reducing the required number of accessible theatre seats).[20] Making performances digitally accessible is not contemplated by the Standards.[21] The law is not written in a way that would allow it to easily expand and grow along with technological development and the availability of new adaptive formats and solutions. An argument could be made that the *spirit* of the ADA requires (or ought to require) theatres to make performances digitally accessible, but that is not the letter of the law, and no such argument has yet been tested in court.

## United Kingdom

In the UK, the rights of the people with disabilities are regulated by the 2010 Equality Act, which establishes a wide range of 'protected characteristics' including disability. As the name of the legislation indicates, the law provides the legal right to be treated equally in all areas of life to people with the protected characteristics.[22] The challenge of the law, as in the US, is in its interpretation. The theatre sector in the UK has so far interpreted it to mean that live performance needs to be wheelchair-accessible on site, but not necessarily accessible to people who can't make it to the venue in person due to their disabilities. Therefore, in the UK at least, since the majority of the performing arts institutions are state-funded, the target for any policy change needs to be not the law (which will never be so specific) but rather the main funding agencies (Arts Council England in particular), who in practice dictate which accessibility elements are a 'must' and which are 'nice to have' in the conditions that they set when they dispense funds.[23]

On its own website, the UK government provides general guidelines to all businesses offering public services:

> Your service must be accessible to everyone who needs it, including services only used by public servants. You may be breaking the law if you do not make your service accessible. You need to think about how users might access and use your service before you design or build anything.

The website further states:

> In the UK, 1 in 5 people have a disability – this could be visual, hearing, motor (affecting fine movement) or cognitive (affecting memory and thinking). The concept of accessibility does not just apply to people with disabilities – all users will have different needs at different times and in different circumstances.[24]

For digital services to meet the government standards, they must 'meet level AA of the Web Content Accessibility Guidelines (WCAG 2.2); work on the most commonly used assistive technologies – including screen magnifiers, screen readers and speech recognition tools; include disabled people in user research; have an accessibility statement that explains how accessible the service is'.[25]

These prescriptions for what accessible digital services should be could potentially be interpreted to mean that legally compliant digital access to performing arts must be a necessary component of government-funded cultural offerings. Moreover, since the law provides specific guides for accessibility of digital content, and requires that certain accessible formats (like books in Braille, for example) must be provided to the disabled patrons of the arts and media, one could reasonably argue that the obligation to provide digital formats for in-person events is already implied in the law. Likewise, since most of the arts programming in the UK is government-funded, the funding agencies can make digital access an essential component of arts funding, designating additional financial resources for that purpose. This, however, has not yet been tested in courts.

### *European Union*

In the European Union,

> The EU's Charter of Fundamental Rights prohibits discrimination on the ground of disability and recognises the right of people with disabilities to benefit from measures to ensure their independence, social and occupational integration and participation in the life of the community. The rights of persons with disabilities in the EU are also protected by the UN Convention on the Rights of Persons with Disabilities (CRPD). In 2010, the EU accepted the CRPD, the first time the EU itself has accepted an international human rights treaty.[26]

Article 7, paragraphs 1 to 4 of the *Directive n° 2010/13/EU of the European Parliament and of the Council of 10 March 2010*, as modified by the Directive n°2018/1808,[27] obligates Member States[28] to require their media service providers to update their accessibility features in line with the progress of technology:

1. Member States shall ensure, without undue delay, that services provided by media service providers under their jurisdiction are made continuously and progressively more accessible to persons with disabilities through proportionate measures.
2. Member States shall ensure that media service providers report on a regular basis to the national regulatory authorities or bodies on the implementation of the measures referred to in paragraph 1. By 19 December 2022 and every three years thereafter, Member States shall report to the Commission on the implementation of paragraph 1.
3. Member States shall encourage media service providers to develop accessibility action plans in respect of continuously and progressively making their services more accessible to persons with disabilities. Any such action plan shall be communicated to national regulatory authorities or bodies.
4. Each Member State shall designate a single, easily accessible, including by persons with disabilities, and publicly available online point of contact for providing information and receiving complaints regarding any accessibility issues referred to in this Article.[29]

As stated in Recital (22) of the 2018/1808 Directive:

> Ensuring the accessibility of audiovisual content is an essential requirement in the context of the commitments taken under the United Nations Convention on the Rights of Persons with Disabilities. … The right of persons with an impairment and of the elderly to participate and be integrated in the social and cultural life of the Union is

> linked to the provision of accessible audiovisual media services. Therefore, Member States should, without undue delay, ensure that media service providers under their jurisdiction actively seek to make content accessible to persons with disabilities, in particular with a visual or hearing impairment. Accessibility requirements should be met through a progressive and continuous process, while taking into account the practical and unavoidable constraints that could prevent full accessibility, such as programmes or events broadcast in real time.[30]

Theatre companies, however, are not audiovisual media services, so in the EU, too, these laws cannot be relied upon to request physical events to be made available in a digital format.

### *Australia*

In Australia, the 1992 Disability Discrimination Act (DDA) (Cth) (CTH stands for Commonwealth of Australia) has similar obligations to those of the US ADA. The DDA

> makes it unlawful to discriminate against a person because of their disability in many areas of public life, including employment, education, getting or using services, renting or buying a house or unit, and accessing public places. The DDA covers people who have temporary and permanent disabilities; physical, intellectual, sensory, neurological, learning and psychosocial disabilities, diseases or illnesses, physical disfigurement, medical conditions, and work-related injuries.[31]

The Arts Access Information Kit developed in 2011 by Live Performance Australia notes that 'It is unlawful in Australia to fail to provide disability access to a public building – including theatres, galleries and concert halls – and failure to do so can result in a discrimination claim being lodged with the

Australian Human Rights Commission ("AHRC").'[32] The law assumes that in the performing arts, physical access and audio descriptions are part of a standard accessibility package. However, it would be hard to imagine that the law would consider it reasonable to expect the performance to be recorded for a disabled person to watch at home. The law would most likely consider such expectation unreasonable, though that assumption has not yet been tested in courts.

## Digital accessibility and copyright laws exceptions

The differences in legal requirements across different countries add to the complexity and clash with the increasingly global and transnational process of theatre-making and distribution. In the US, the situation is particularly complicated, as many professional performing arts unions, including SAG-AFTRA (The Screen Actors Guild–American Federation of Television and Radio Artists) and the Actors' Equity Association, stipulate that any use of show footage requires a special non-broadcast agreement. These requirements often conflict with the accessibility needs of marginalized audiences who cannot access cultural offerings in person. Likewise, the exceptions to copyright laws are often vague or insufficient to enforce any sort of human rights compliance. Rather than create paths to solidarity between the audience members with disabilities and often equally marginalized theatre workers, the legal discourse defines the relationship as fundamentally adversary.

### *United States*

In the US, it is common for playwrights or other copyright holders to grant theatres only the right to present a live stage production of their play with living actors appearing in the immediate presence of an in-person audience at a specified physical venue beginning on a specified date and ending on a specified date. The copyright holder may deny theatres permission to create a digital version of the same production for distribution via streaming or download.

The Chafee Amendment presents one possible model for creating a copyright exemption for theatres seeking to expand digital accessibility for audience members with disabilities.[33] In 1996, Republican senator John Chafee introduced a bill that would allow authorized entities to reproduce or distribute copies or phonorecords of previously published literary or musical works in accessible formats exclusively for use by people with disabilities. Signed into law by President Clinton that same year, the legislation was inspired by the free national library programme of reading materials for print-disabled individuals, which was established in 1931. The programme was initially dependent on the cooperation of individual copyright holders who granted permission to create special format reproductions of their works without paying a royalty. The Chafee Amendment removed this limitation and vastly expanded accessibility.

In *Authors Guild, Inc. v Hathi Trust*, a federal appellate court relied in part on the Chafee Amendment in holding that the copyright 'fair use' doctrine allowed research libraries to create a full-text searchable database of copyrighted works and to provide those works in formats accessible to people with disabilities.[34] While the Chafee Amendment itself is likely too narrowly drafted to provide standalone support for expanding the right to digitally accessible performances, the *Authors Guild* case suggests that courts are willing to construe the Act somewhat expansively when confronted with new technological applications.

The economic damage done to the nonprofit theatre sector by the COVID-19 pandemic prompted federal lawmakers to introduce legislation aimed at reviving the industry. Recognizing that theatres across the country were struggling financially in the wake of the pandemic due to inflation and diminished audiences for in-person performances, Democratic senators Peter Welch, John Fetterman, and Jack Reed recently sponsored the Supporting Theater and the Arts to Galvanize the Economy (STAGE) Act of 2024. If passed into law, the legislation would allocate $1 billion that theatres could use for basic operating expenses, including the costs associated with payroll, rent or mortgage payments, and building sets and costumes. A theatre recently found to have violated Title I of the Americans with Disabilities Act would not be eligible for STAGE Act funding.[35]

The bill also provides that theatres could use the funds for

> [c]osts associated with the improvement, repair, or maintenance of an existing facility housing theatrical productions, projects, performances, workshops, or programs, with priority given to costs for upgrades necessary for fully accessible workplaces for professional performers and related or supporting professional personnel with disabilities ... or [o]ther uses, as determined by the Secretary [of Commerce].[36]

The bill does not explicitly provide funding for theatres to put toward expanding digital accessibility for audience members with disabilities, but its sponsors are clearly attuned to the needs of people with disabilities, as evidenced by the provision of the bill referenced before and Senator Fetterman's public lived experience with disability. Before the bill becomes law, lawmakers should clarify that STAGE Act funding may be used for this purpose. New federal legislation directly addressing the theatre industry is exceedingly rare, and this bill may be the last opportunity advocates have for many years to effect nationwide change.

### *United Kingdom*

Following the ratification of the Marrakesh VIP Treaty in 2013,[37] in the UK the Copyright, Designs and Patents Act 1988 (CDPA) provides two exceptions to its copyright law under Sections 31A–31F (which was added in 2014) in order to facilitate access to culture for the people with disabilities.[38]

The first exception permits a person with disability or their representative to make a copy, without seeking permission, of copyrighted material (such as book or video) for personal use in a format necessary for access appropriate for the person's disability (making a copy of a book in Braille, for example). The second exception permits 'educational establishments and charity organisations to make, communicate, make available, distribute and lend accessible format-copies of protected works on behalf of disabled people'.[39] The second exception allows for:

> making Braille, audio or large-print copies of books, newspapers or magazines for visually impaired people
>
> adding audio-description to films or broadcasts for visually impaired people
>
> making subtitled films or broadcasts for deaf or hard of hearing people
>
> making accessible copies of books, newspapers or magazines for dyslexic people.[40]

The law places restrictions on how the copies can be made and distributed and by whom. These include:

> accessible copies of copyright protected works can be made only from lawfully accessed copies.
>
> an accessible copy can only be made by a disabled person or an authorised body acting on their behalf.
>
> the copy can only be made for the personal use of a disabled person. Accessible copies cannot be made, communicated, made available, distributed or lent to a person that is not a disabled person under these exceptions.
>
> bodies that make, communicate, make available, distribute and lend accessible copies must fulfil the

definition of an 'authorised body' outlined in Section 31F CDPA.

an accessible copy must only change a copyright work to the extent that is necessary to convert it to an accessible format.

the making, communicating, making available, distributing or lending of an accessible copy by an authorised body must be done on a non-profit basis. This means that, for example, an authorised body must not make a profit when they make and distribute an accessible copy of a book.[41]

Although the law allows for making of accessible copies of films and videos, it does not mention whether the video recording itself can be considered an accessible 'format'. However, if we consider a live performance as a form of original text, which is a standard understanding in theatre and performance theory,[42] then, in legal terms, based on the existing exceptions to the UK copyright laws, the recording of a live performance could be considered a form of accessible format, which then nonprofit organizations could be required theoretically to provide to patrons who are unable to access the live performance in person (in the same way they are required to provide wheelchair ramps). Section 31A.1b states that making an accessible copy should be done in cases when 'the person's disability prevents the person from enjoying the work to the same degree as a person who does not have that disability'.[43] People with disabilities, the immunocompromised, and the chronically ill individuals (including those who suffer from long COVID) are prevented by their disabilities from enjoying the work in the same way that their nondisabled fellow citizens can. Recoded copies of such events would ameliorate that disadvantage.

Furthermore, requiring the performing arts organizations to provide digital formats of their shows would necessarily require the funding agencies to provide economic support for that process that would be sufficient to cover all associated costs. One could argue that the copyright exceptions allow for reproduction of an existing recording of a show and are not a legal obligation placed on the institutions to make the first fixation (the first recording).[44] However, this interpretation of the law would make it impossible to make a copy of a book in Braille, as it could be theoretically viewed as a 'first fixation'. It would also put into question the organization's obligations to provide any disability accommodations (including wheelchair ramps and lifts to their buildings). As it is written, the current UK exceptions, which derive from the Marrakesh VIP Treaty, place the financial burden of making an accessible format (making a Braille copy of an existing book, for example) on the disabled person (or the proxy acting on their behalf). As mentioned earlier, this is inconsistent with other obligations imposed under disability laws that put the financial obligations of making public places and places of business accessible on the businesses and funding bodies. Thus, there is a misalignment in how different types of accessibility are treated under the law. While physical accessibility (like wheelchair ramps and lifts, for example) is the responsibility of the business or public space, the accessibility of content (like books or performances) is often left to individual or third-party nonprofit organizations acting on their behalf. In that sense, the entire framing of the accessibility of content as a function of copyright exception is misaligned with other disability laws.[45]

### *European Union*

In the EU, responding to the need for updated copyright laws, in November 2022 the European Theatre Convention released *Performing Arts Recordings and Broadcasts: A Practical Manual on Author's and Related Rights*, written by Maxime de Brogniez and Antoine Vandenbulke, EU copyright experts at the University of Liège, and the University of Mons – Free University of Brussels (Belgium), who identified 'the various legal issues that arise across Europe when recording performances and broadcasting them online'. The manual 'offers practical advice on writing contracts to address these challenges in a simple way'. The goal of the manual is to 'help people working in theatre and the performing arts broadcast recorded performances online'.[46,47] Indeed, the audiovisual broadcast of a live performance (previously recorded or broadcast live) raises new copyright issues that are not (or less) relevant when a play is confined to the theatre.

First, the online distribution of a live show is likely to reach a much larger audience over a much broader territory and, therefore, to draw attention to possible breaches on author's rights that would not necessarily be noticed in the context of a performance played in a theatre. From a legal point of view, the infringement exists in both situations, but it is more likely to be sanctioned when the performance is broadcast on other channels, such as television or online. A cease-and-desist order may therefore be filed to stop the infringement and possible damages may be claimed.

Then, the recording of a play requires theatres to take into consideration *neighbouring rights* in addition to those of the authors. Indeed, when actors perform on stage or musicians interpret a score, their intellectual property rights are very limited (unless they are also authors of the text or composers of the score, for example). In fact, their main effective rights are the possibility of preventing the broadcast or the recording of their performances.[48] As soon as the performance is recorded, artists can fully assert their so-called neighbouring rights or related rights to copyright (considered synonyms) on their fixed performance; so that producers must obtain their authorization to reproduce or communicate (for example, online) the recorded play. Online broadcast requires, therefore, the authorization of the holders of these related rights. Indeed, an actor who agrees to perform on stage can object that the play – which has been recorded – is then distributed online. In addition to obtaining the authorizations from the copyright holders, the producer must also obtain the necessary authorizations from the holders of related rights.[49]

The third issue raised by the audiovisual broadcasting of performing arts concerns the assessment of – or the license for – the different modes of exploitation. Licenses or assignments of copyright and related rights must be made in written form and are strictly interpreted – a copyrighted work may only be exploited in those forms explicitly named in license agreements or assignments. For example, the authorization to use a piece of music in a performance does not imply *per se* the authorization to incorporate the same music in a recording (unless the contract expressly authorizes it). This has caused confusion in the theatre sector,[50] especially for plays that were not originally intended to be broadcast online or on television – which, due to the pandemic, became the only way to stay connected to the audience.

The consequences of this confusion can be significant, since a single missing authorization can block the entire project. For example, if authorization to use a piece of music in the context of a broadcast has not been granted, the rightful owner may oppose the broadcast of this music, which would leave the producer with two options: to distribute the scene without the music or to cut the scenes containing this music. Nevertheless, in these two cases, it is possible that some rights holders (for example, the stage director) would claim their moral right, in particular the right to the integrity of the work, in order to object to substantial changes to their work.

The duration and territory of the assignment or license must also be clearly identified. The issue of territory is becoming increasingly crucial in the case of online broadcast, since the performance is no longer limited by physical borders.

Furthermore, since the 2019 Directive,[51] European law requires that the authors and performers who license or assign their exclusive rights to use their works have the right to an *appropriate and proportional* remuneration at the actual or potential value of the rights that are granted under license or are assigned.[52,53] Recital 73 of the Directive then specifies that '[a] lump sum payment can also constitute proportionate remuneration', but it should not be the rule. The Directive specifies, however, that the authors may authorize their works to be used for free.[54]

The European Union directives on copyright law provide provisions for disability access. *Directive 2001/29/EC of the European Parliament and of the Council of 22 May 2001 on the Harmonisation of Certain Aspects of Copyright and Related Rights in the Information Society* specifies that exceptions to copyright law can be made on the basis of disability:

> Member States may provide for exceptions or limitations to the rights provided for in Articles 2 and 3 in the following cases: … (b) uses, for the benefit of people with a disability, which are directly related to the disability and of a non-commercial nature, to the extent required by the specific disability. (Article 5)[55]

In European Union law, directives are legislative instruments which must be transposed by all the Member States into their national legislation, *via* a law or other appropriate instrument. While certain provisions must necessarily be incorporated into national law, the 2001/29/EC Directive leaves a wide margin of discretion to Member States regarding exceptions to copyright. Thus, the general exception for disabled people is only an option for European Union Member States, not an obligation, even though Recital 43 of the Directive stresses the importance of making access possible for disabled people.[56] The exception does not impose positive responsibility on the Member States, but it makes it possible to derogate from the copyright law in order to address accessibility needs of the disabled person within the limited scope, specific to the national laws.

Note that, in order to comply with the Treaty of Marrakesh, Directive (UE) 2017/1564[57] imposes a mandatory exception, that all Member States must implement, to facilitate the access to certain works for people who are blind, visually impaired or otherwise print disabled. If this exception mainly concerns writing, such as books or newspapers, it also extends to audiobooks and therefore applies to related rights – recorded plays are, nevertheless, not directly concerned by this directive. This secondary legislation aims to ensure that beneficiary persons have access to books and other printed material in accessible formats across the EU internal market. The directive indeed authorizes beneficiary persons (or authorized entities) to make an accessible format copy of those works for their personal use; authorized entities are also entitled 'to communicate, make available, distribute or lend an accessible format copy to a beneficiary person or another authorised entity on a non-profit basis for the purpose of exclusive use by a beneficiary person'.[58]

### *Case study: Poland*

The Central and Eastern European countries present an interesting case study, illustrating the complexity of the EU copyright laws from a vantage point rooted in historical and economic circumstances that differ from those established in Western Europe and the US. Poland in particular might provide an instructive theoretical model for resolving the many tensions embedded in the challenges of digital access. Before World War I, the Russian, Prussian, and Austro-Hungarian empires that emerged in the eighteenth century partitioned and eventually came to dominate the smaller Central and Eastern European nations (including Poland, Ukraine, and Bohemia, among others). In Poland, with public institutions controlled by colonizers, theatre became central to the process of creating the idea of a nation. Following World War I, when Poland regained its independence, theatre and opera continued to be essential to nation-building as a platform for the reconstitution, enactment, and solidification of a sense of shared national discourse and identity. Following World War II, during the Soviet occupation of the region, the communist governments drew on these strong prewar theatrical traditions, funding theatre and arts as a tool of both internal and international propaganda.[59] Thus, Central and Eastern European countries developed a long-standing tradition of digitizing and producing new theatre for television (and radio). Production and dissemination of theatre by the state was an important part of social access and a vital political project.

In Poland, the communist government supported 'the Polish theatre, never stinting it money or other means'.[60] Theatre was also 'an export' product meant to enhance Poland's international reputation, promoting 'Polish culture abroad, [while masking] communist power by showing its "human face"'.[61] While tightly censored and controlled by the state, theatre also became a form of escape, a space where unspoken truths could be delivered in between lines and whispers. Well-funded Theatre TV programming – a weekly showing of theatre productions – has been running on Polish television since 1953 (the year of Stalin's death) and, until 2013, ran as a repertoire theatre on free-to-air channels. It still runs on free-to-air channels and produces new works (some streamed live) several times a year. In addition, Theatre TV also digitizes the most significant productions for broadcasting to wider audiences.[62] The most recent example is the musical *1989* (one of the most discussed shows of 2022), which was livestreamed via Theatre TV in May 2024, free and available to anyone with a television set. The data showed that 824,000 people watched it live when it streamed on Monday, 27 May 2024, at 8 pm. This is a significant audience. For comparison, in March 2024, the main evening news programme at 7:30 pm on the Polish public TV channel was watched by 1,346,202 people.[63] In addition to the Theatre TV archive, the Polish state also maintains a free streaming database of selected Theatre TV shows (now funded by the EU), some of which are available with English subtitles.[64]

Following the fall of the Berlin Wall in 1989, Polish theatre lost its footing for a while. No longer as politically necessary and well-funded as during communism, theatre was searching for new social and political models, emerging eventually as a mediating space between Polish society and its democratically elected, if not always beloved governments. However, despite the long-standing tradition of recording and streaming theatre through Theatre TV, when the COVID-19 pandemic broke – especially before special government funding was allocated – Polish theatre felt unprepared for digital engagement. The staff had no technical expertise or tools (programmes, cameras, and so on). Many initial initiatives were actor-led, streamed from private homes, and built on individual digital literacy. The division of labour across the departments was also unclear. Was it the responsibility of the technical or marketing department, for example, to organize theatre streams?[65] Tickets were either free or much cheaper than regular tickets for in-person shows, which had an immediate negative effect on institutional finances. But the encouraging change in attitude to be more positive towards online theatre came with the introduction of appropriate funding, and with time and practice, the quality of and excitement about engaging online technologies in theatre increased.[66] The main activities in Poland included archival streams, mini theatre projects (such as the National Theatre's *Poeci Polscy* [Polish Poets]), livestreamed smaller forms (with small casts) performed on the stage without audiences and with the COVID precautions changing the choreography of the shows, and new digital experiments with Zoom and other telematic digital technologies.[67]

Focusing specifically on Poland, Maria Babicka and Justyna Czarnota coordinated extensive research (published in 2021) at Poland's Theatre Institute on the theatre's responses to the pandemic. Their research covered such areas as the presence of theatres online, institutional initiatives, theatre criticism, theatre employees, audience, artists, and amateur/nonprofessional theatre (which is an important element of

Poland's theatre ecosystem). In all these contexts, the study showed that the online presence and digital activities of theatres invited new thinking about live performance in relation to its funding structures, theatre criticism, practices of theatre-making, engagement with communities, new theatre forms, and aesthetics.[68]

The 2021 study by Anna Buchner, Katarzyna Fereniec-Błońska, Katarzyna Kalinowska, and Maria Wierzbicka examined the ways in which the internet both changes and benefits theatre, focusing on individual theatre institutions, employees responsible for online engagement, and audiences. Through qualitative interviews with 41 respondents representing the three different contexts, they observed that the increased-through-pandemic presence of theatres online and their digital activities led to increased engagement with audience development from individual institutions. With online audiences now spread across geographic locations, developing engaged and growing viewership for theatre started to be perceived as a collaborative effort shared across different theatre institutions. The study also showed that the groups attending theatres live and those engaged online were not the same people, although they of course share common characteristics. Spectators who previously had no access to theatre – whether because of health, family situation, or social exclusion – engaged with online productions.[69] The introduction of new audiences to theatre through its online presence was also a finding of Bogna Kietlińska's survey-based research focused on spectators conducted in April and May 2020. The importance of the online theatre for spectators was underpinned by its flexible viewing options, the agency over one's engagement it offered, accessibility, and inclusivity around different needs and practices of cultural participation, breaking the financial and social barriers.[70]

Pandemic-era online theatre also revealed the gaps in copyright and labour law.[71] With the financial impact that the lockdowns had on artists, the gap in Polish copyright law became apparent. One of the respondents in the Polish Theatre Institute's project summed it up well: 'A theatrical performance in my translation and three readings of my translated plays were presented online, on the YouTube platform. One of them has so far been watched by more than 213,000 viewers, the others – well over 50,000. The activities mentioned earlier brought me an income of 0.00 PLN.'[72]

The online performances were not protected by copyright law. This linked with the EU-wide discussion on the EU artists' copyright and *neighbouring rights* or *related rights* to copyright. In the Polish context, this became the foundation of a national debate, and a new law on digital rights and fees was legislated in September 2024. It is partly an outcome of the public debate and partly an implementation of the EU 2019 copyright directives (2019/789 and 2019/790) related to copyright and online transmissions and the Digital Single Market. Poland is the last EU country to implement this directive.[73] The important law extends copyright law into the realm of the internet. After pressure from artists and unions, the Polish government added to the national implementation of the EU law additional protections for the artists. The new legislation introduces royalties for making and disseminating audiovisual works publicly so people can access them at a time and place of their choosing. As demanded by artists and unions, the fees are negotiated by collective management agencies such as Związek Artystów Scen Polskich (ZASP, the Union of Poland's Stage Artists).[74] The artists also gain rights to royalties for rebroadcasting of the artistic works by streaming platforms, VOD, and cable.[75]

Previously in Poland, royalties were paid by media companies for rebroadcasting of audiovisual and audio works on free-to-air channels. For example, Polish National Television (TVP) paid artists for making works for Theatre TV. This happened even if the work had already been created for live performance and was adapted for Theatre TV. However, Theatre TV was also obliged to pay artists for rebroadcasting of such works. The rates were negotiated with the artists or the collective management agencies that represent them. For theatre-makers this has been normally ZASP.[76] It was the responsibility of the broadcaster to submit the list of works they have been showing to the appropriate collective management agency together with the day and time of each broadcast. This was checked by the agency, and calculations of fees are made based on that list. ZASP, for example, has created a calculation system based on points that depend on the type of role an actor plays (lead, secondary, and so on), time of broadcasting, and type and length of the work. The points for a specific work were multiplied by how many times the work was broadcasted. The points translated to the fee received by an actor.[77] The rates per point were different for different broadcasters. For example, they were smaller for the cultural television channel because of the cultural and social value of such broadcasts. Actors and unions successfully fought for the same obligations to be put on the VOD and streaming platforms and on subscription-based television programmes, so that their work and rights are appropriately valued and remunerated.[78]

The Polish example shows that a high level of state-based support that views theatre in a national context as a public good can go hand in hand with a high level of protection of the rights holders in theatre pieces. Due to its historical model of state-based support that views theatre in the national context as a public good, Poland's existing social infrastructure and tradition of recording and distributing live theatre via its television channels allowed for the development of straightforward, universal standards of access that do not compromise artists' rights. In order for a similar model to be developed in the West, which would treat recording and distribution of theatre as given, both public and private funding needs to start considering such an approach as necessary, prioritizing support for the archivization and distribution of theatre works across the national cultural landscapes.

### Australia

In Australia, the 'Sculpting a National Cultural Plan' report, published in 2020, notes the digital copyright exemptions as barriers to digital pivoting, how Australia differs from some other jurisdictions, and what can be done to address the Australian deficiencies.

> Future-proofing and the ability to pivot were highlighted in evidence from the Australian Libraries and Copyright Committee (ALCC) and the Australian Digital Alliance (ADA). The ALCC and the ADA drew attention to flexible copyright laws as an enabler for innovation. In considering current Australian copyright law, their joint submission raised concern that: 'Australian law permits the use of certain material without a license for "research or study," "criticism or review," or "reporting the news" among other purposes which serve the public interest. However, the list of purposes for which copyright material may be used is rigid and ill-suited to the modern age where innovative new uses are being developed all the time. Unless an activity falls within one of the fixed categories of allowable uses under the Act, it is prohibited.' [Submission 32][79]

Professor David Throsby, Dr Jan Zwar, and Dr Paul Crosby suggested extending the Public Lending Right (PLR) and Educational Lending Right (ELR) schemes, which presently ensure that Australian authors are paid for their work when lent from libraries: 'One practical policy initiative would be to recognise the digital component of book borrowing by extending PLR and ELR payments to include digital lending by libraries [Submission 34].'[80]

In December 2022, the Australian Government's Copyright Enforcement Review issued a paper which includes a submission from the Australian Libraries and Archives Copyright Coalition (ALACC), advocating for copyright law reform in the interests of Australian libraries, archives, and information providers. ALACC also deals with issues affecting people with disabilities.[81] ALACC's submission to the Copyright Enforcement Review touched on problems with the current 'safe harbour' scheme:

> The introduction of the *Copyright Amendment (Service Providers) Act 2018*[82] extended the definition of an ISP to include cultural, educational and disability groups where they provide certain services to the public. Cultural and educational institutions in particular welcomed this extension as it provides certainty in the provisions of online services that include content uploaded by third parties. We support the continued inclusion of cultural and educational institutions, as well as disability organisations, within the operation of the safe harbour scheme. … The copyright safe harbours balance the rights of copyright owners, copyright users and service providers in a way that supports innovative creation of new offerings. Expanding the copyright safe harbour to all online service providers, consistent with international peer markets, would level the playing field for Australian platforms and provide legislative underpinning for existing notice and take-down schemes.[83]

In addition to the House of Representatives report and news stories, there are other published materials on the arts-related impacts of the COVID pandemic on Australians with disabilities, some focusing on the ways in which copyright law can function as a barrier. These include the 'Copyright Enforcement Review' (2022); the WIPO report on the impacts of COVID on the creative industries and institutions (2022), which includes Australia; Arts Access Australia's set of best practice Principles; and the Storytime Agreement between Australian publishers and library representatives.

In 2022, WIPO published a report titled 'The Impact of the COVID-19 Pandemic on Creative Industries, Cultural Institutions, Education and Research', which came from the Information Session on the Impact of the COVID-19 Pandemic on the Copyright Ecosystem, held on 9 May 2022, during the 42nd Session of the Standing Committee on Copyright and Related Rights (SCCR). One contribution was from the Australian Government's Arts COVID Recovery and Response Team. This short document was a filled-in form that had been sent to participants by WIPO, and it doesn't specifically mention disability. It gives an example of action taken by the Australian Government.

In August 2020, the Australian Government announced proposed reforms to simplify and update Australia's copyright laws to better support and align the use of copyright material in the physical and digital environments, while copyright holders continue to be fairly remunerated for the use of their material. These proposed reforms are primarily targeted at sectors that serve important public interests, including the cultural and education sectors. While the issues addressed by the proposed reforms are not new, the importance of an adaptable copyright framework was highlighted during the COVID-19 pandemic, with the transition to widespread online and remote learning and online delivery of many public institutions' services, and the impacts of the pandemic on the creative sector.[84]

The CRPD creates a right to access cultural materials and helps reduce the barriers that intellectual property laws can create in providing access to such cultural performances. Illustratively, CRPD article 30(1)(b) grants persons with disabilities a right to take part in cultural life, including theatre, on an equal basis with others. Prior to the CRPD, but for limited exceptions, such as the Berne three-step-test, international intellectual property laws have historically prioritized commercial copyright interests over information access for persons with disabilities.[85] The UN Convention on the Rights of Persons with Disabilities article 30(3) provides that States Parties shall take all appropriate steps, in accordance with international law, to ensure that laws protecting intellectual property rights do not constitute an unreasonable or discriminatory barrier to access by persons with disabilities to cultural materials. Article 30(3) of the CRPD has been used by disability rights advocates to successfully champion shifts in intellectual property laws at the domestic and international levels. Examples of these shifts can be evidenced at the national level, by the prioritizing of disability access by the South African Constitutional Court[86] and, internationally, by the World Property Organization adopting the Marrakesh Treaty to Facilitate Access to Published Works for Persons Who Are Blind, Visually Impaired, or Otherwise Print Disabled, opened for signature 28 June 2013, WIPO Doc VIP/DC/8 (30 September 2016) [hereinafter the Marrakesh Treaty].[87] The intellectual property paradigm prior to the CRPD placed IP above disability access to information. Art 30(3) of the CRPD is paradigm-shifting, in that it reduces the primacy of IP law. This has led to the WIPO adopting the Marrakesh Treaty, which further entrenches the relevance of disability access to information.[88]

## Copyright laws vs disability rights

In his article 'Copyright and Disability' (2021), Blake Ellis Reid points out that where there is a conflict between copyright laws and disability rights laws, the copyright interests always take priority. It is assumed that disability rights will be secondary, and the needs of the people with disabilities subjugated to the needs of the copyright holders. This is not the case with the civil rights of other protected groups. Reid writes:

> copyright's ableist tradition subordinates the actual interests of people with disabilities to access copyrighted works to the hypothetical interests of copyright holders who may withhold access without reason. This subordination has led to a harmful, invasive, and unnecessary intrusion of copyright's permission structure and culture into disability policy.[89]

Reid further argues

> that copyright limitations and exceptions should not be understood as an expansion of access to people with disabilities but rather as an important-but-modest reversal of copyright's largely unnecessary presence in disability policy. That reversal leaves unresolved significant questions about how to actually make copyrighted works accessible that must ultimately be answered by disability law, not copyright law.[90]

By shifting the debate in a way that prioritizes disability law over copyright law, Reid proposes a paradigm shift in the way we conceptualize access. As Eric Johnson has argued, 'American intellectual property law has, as a general matter, proceeded in ignorance of disabilities.'[91] Rethinking that legal tradition requires acknowledging that disabled people's right to access cultural products is part of a broader, international civil and human rights debate in which access to culture is viewed as a necessary component of civic participation, social inclusion, and public health. Reid concludes: 'It can be counterintuitive that copyright law can pose a barrier to making creative works accessible when obligations to make copyrighted works accessible are a significant component of both human and civil rights regimes in international and U.S. disability law.'[92] For the performing arts, the shift in prioritizing access over copyright claims also means that the needs of disabled audience members would be considered and funded on par with those of nondisabled audience members. This approach, however, requires a fundamental restructuring of how governments and private institutions support and fund art making and art distribution.

# FIVE

# Recommendations

## Research and digital library access

Like the New York Public Library for the Performing Arts, the Strong Museum of Play in Rochester, New York, which houses an extensive collection of video games, provides access to its archive only when a person can physically travel there and play the games onsite. In recent years, game researchers, preservationists, and historians, represented by the Software Preservation Network and the Library Copyright Alliance, have been lobbying the Copyright Office to create additional exceptions to the Digital Millennium Copyright Act (DMCA), which would allow for temporary remote online access to the various video game archives, thus eliminating the problem of travel and making the Strong Museum and other video game collections available to broader group of researchers.[1]

In April 2024, the Software Preservation Network and the Library Copyright Alliance argued in front of the Copyright Office for a model of 'individualized human review' of the access requests that would allow researchers and other legitimate parties remote access to the collections 'primarily for the purposes of private study, scholarship, teaching, or research'.[2] During the Copyright Office hearing, NYU professor Laine Nooney, who represented the researchers, argued that the need to travel to an onsite location to access the video game collection presents 'a significant financial and logistical impediment to doing research'.[3] Consequently, due to the costs and time commitment that travel requires, research access is limited to those with sufficient social and economic privilege. The opposing counsel, Robert Rothstein, the lawyer representing the video game industry, offered a counterargument. The industry opposes adding the additional research exceptions to the copyright law on the grounds that it could facilitate entertainment use of the collections. Rothstein insisted that an issue is more of a 'travel problem' (possibly resolved with more research funding) and not a legal problem in need of resolution.

On 25 October 2024, the US Copyright Office sided with the video game industry and has refused a request for a DMCA exemption that would permit libraries to share access to video games collections remotely for research and archival purposes: 'Under the current anti-circumvention rules in Section 1201 of the DMCA, libraries and archives are unable to break copy protection on games in order to make them remotely accessible to researchers.'[4] The Copyright ruling was based on the assumption that the access for research purposes would likely infringe on copyright laws: 'The Register concludes that proponents did not show that removing the single-user limitation for preserved computer programs or permitting off-premises access to video games are likely to be noninfringing.'[5] In other words, the remote access to video games would not qualify as legal 'fair use'. The Register 'also notes the greater risk of market harm with removing the video game exemption's premises limitation, given the market for legacy video games'.[6]

Notably, in his argument in favour of the exception, among the reasons listed for potential travel challenges, such as finances, time, and resources, Nooney does not mention disabilities, and the hearing never considers ADA law as a valid basis for access request. The video game case with its broadly defined access needs can serve as a model for the re-evaluating of DMCA rules with regard to performing arts and disability laws. The difference between the two arguments – one in favour of access for the purpose of more equitable research, and one in favour of access due to disabilities – lies in their target audience and purpose. The video game case rests on the assumption that access would be provided for a limited time and purpose to a limited number of individuals whose professional identities and objectives would undergo a stringent review before being granted digital access. The ADA-based argument posits that one has a right to access the digital archives of cultural artefacts for any reason, including entertainment, based solely on one's disability needs.

Similar case, *Hachette v Internet Archive*, have recently made its way through the US courts with regards to the Internet Archive, known for its open-access policy and the commitment to free dissemination of knowledge. In March 2020, the Archive initiated a digital library programme called the National Emergency Library, or NEL, with the goal of replacing physical libraries that were closed during the COVID-19 restrictions. The NEL programme was based on the Archive's Open Library project, which has been lending scanned books since 2006, lending out one digital copy for each physical copy the Archive owned. The NEL programme expanded the digital lending programme, by enabling unlimited simultaneous access to each scanned book the Archive owned. The move prompted a strong online backlash and forced the Archive to roll back this expansion of access, but the uproar resulted in immediate response from the four major US publishers including Hachette Book Group and Penguin Random House, which sued the Archive challenging the practice of digitizing and lending books from its Open Library collection, on the basis that digital lending violates the copyright, and does not fall under the fair use exception.

The Internet Archive's legal battle over digital book lending practices reached a critical juncture in September 2024 when the US Court of Appeals for the 2nd Circuit upheld a lower court's ruling against the nonprofit organization. While the Internet Archive maintained that its Open Library operated similarly to traditional libraries by lending one digital copy for each physical copy owned, the Court determined this practice was not protected under fair use doctrine, and in fact violated copyright law. The ruling emphasized that accepting the Archive's interpretation of fair use would substantially weaken copyright owners' exclusive rights to prepare derivative works and potentially undermine the publishing industry's financial stability. In fact, the Court called the Archive's argument in favour of the fair use exception 'unpersuasive'. Maria A. Pallante, the president of the Association of American Publishers responded to the Court's ruling, praising the decision: 'If there was any doubt, the Court makes clear that under fair use jurisprudence there is nothing transformative about converting entire works into new formats without permission or appropriating the value of derivative works that are a key part of the author's copyright bundle.'[7]

The Internet Archive case, like the gaming archive case of the Strong Museum of Play, highlights the ongoing tension between expanding public access to knowledge and protecting intellectual property rights. Although the Internet Archive argued that its scanning practices were transformational and thus protected under fair use doctrine, the Court's decision has established significant precedent regarding the limits of digital library services and their relationship with traditional publishing models. Both cases highlight the strong copyright protections that make digital access to culture difficult for people with disabilities, the elderly, and other economically and geographically marginalized groups.

One potentially instructive model for legally viable digital access to cultural products can be found in the National Library Service's BARD (Braille and Audio Reading Download) system.[8] BARD provides eligible readers who are blind, visually impaired, physically handicapped, or print disabled with access to over 125,000 digital audio and braille books, magazines, and music materials. BARD, which launched in 2009, is based on the collection of the National Library Service for the Blind and Print Disabled (NLS), which was initially founded in 1932 as

'Project, Books for the Adult Blind'.[9] Unlike the video game case, which revolves around copyright exception based on fair use for research purposes, and unlike the Internet Archive case, which attempted to classify digital lending under fair use exception, BARD has successfully implemented fair use doctrine based on ADA law by developing a secure digital access system that balances copyright protection with accessibility needs. Through individual authentication and stringent eligibility verification, BARD ensures that only qualified disabled patrons can access its digital collections. 'Eligibility of Blind and Other Physically Handicapped Persons' must be verified by the qualified medical professional. BARD's definition of the eligible person includes patrons with physical disabilities who are 'unable to read or unable to use regular printed material because of physical limitations'.[10] This definition can potentially include not just patrons whose disabilities are limited to various vision-related impairments, but also those whose physical disabilities might prevent them from being able to access the physical libraries.

The BARD model demonstrates how institutions can provide broad digital access to its disabled patrons while maintaining strict control over the distribution of its collection, and thus ensuring they don't fall afoul the copyright laws. BARD system allows users to download content directly to their devices, eliminating the need for physical travel while still protecting copyright holders' interests through encrypted files and controlled distribution. BARD's success suggests that similar authentication and distribution models could be adapted for performing arts institutions, libraries, and archives, allowing homebound patrons with disabilities to access theatrical recordings without compromising copyright protections or requiring physical presence at the location.

## Archivization and AI

The problem of digital access also inevitably raises a wide range of questions related to the ethics and politics of digitizing and archiving of culture. Whose culture is digitalized, archived, and made available for future generations to research and view, and under what circumstances? In other words, whose culture, how, when, and why, is designated as representative of the national culture worthy of preserving and archiving? Typically, the holdings of the national digital archives of film, television, and performing arts centre on historically dominant, privileged, mainstream culture. Digital national open-access theatre archives such as France's Madelen[11] or Poland's Ninateka[12] are databases of classic productions, effectively serving as time capsules of a particular era in French and Polish cultures.

In his short articles published in *The Guardian* in May 2024, Jason Okundaye chronicles his 'hunt' for the 1991 British Channel 4 episodes of *The Black Bag*, a TV series about Black experience in the UK. Okundaye was specifically looking for an episode focused on Black gay lives of the era for his book on the topic of gay culture. Finding that episode, however, proved to be a challenge, since neither 'Channel 4's own digital archive and the BFI's free Black Britain on Film collection' had the episode in question in their holdings.[13] The anecdote underscores the exclusionary practices that have traditionally underpinned many of the historical archiving processes.

With the emergence of AI and new digital research practices such as data visualization, network analysis, and text mining, the content of an archive is no longer just a site of national identity and cultural memory (as Diana Taylor notes[14]), but it is also a site of future epistemologies that might potentially encompass all aspects of our lives. For this reason alone, a comprehensive documentation and digitization of our performance cultures, in all their diverse and wide-ranging forms, is imperative and should be supported not only by state and nonprofit funders but by the AI companies themselves. The tech companies should not just rely on existing historical archives for their data but should fund the processes of archiving and digitization of current cultures.

There are many copyright issues connected to generative AI that make deliberate and lawful archivization such an imperative.[15] In 2023, the Copyright Office has initiated the process of figuring out what type of AI-generated artwork could be copyrighted. The problem became even more complicated when the author claimed the use of AI not as a generative tool, but as an assistive technology. In 2024, the Copyright Office relented and registered an AI-generated book submitted by a disabled author with cognitive impairment, establishing a precedent.[16]

In January 2025, following nearly two years of inquiry, the Copyright Office finally issued a report on 'Copyright and Artificial Intelligence. Part 2: Copyrightability', which concluded that 'The use of AI tools to assist rather than stand in for human creativity does not affect the availability of copyright protection for the output', and 'Copyright protects the original expression in a work created by a human author, even if the work also includes AI-generated material'.[17] In other words, the human creativity involved in AI-assisted work can be copyrighted. In Section IVB of the document, specifically titled 'Empowering Creators with Disabilities', the Copyright asserted that

> to the extent these functionalities [of AI] are used as tools to recast, transform, or adapt an author's expression, copyright protection would be available for the resulting work. … The distinction between assistive uses and generative ones applies equally to creators with disabilities and other human authors. Copyright protection remains available where AI functions as an assistive tool that allows human authors to express their creativity.[18]

When used as an assistive tool for creators with disabilities, AI-generated works can be copyrightable. At the same time, the Copyright Office concluded that works generated with prompts alone cannot be copyrighted: 'the capabilities of the latest generative A.I. technologies raise challenging questions about the nature and scope of human authorship. … Prompts alone, however, at this stage are unlikely to satisfy those requirements'.[19]

In 2025, in the first major AI copyright lawsuit between Thomson Reuters (RT, media company) and Ross Intelligence (RI, AI company), the judge ruled in favour of TR, arguing that the use of its archive by RI was not subject to 'fair use' doctrine.[20] At the same time, Invoke, a generative AI platform, received first copyright protection for an AI-assisted image.[21] Complex copyright guidelines and rulings like this increasingly underscore the need for legally viable data sets for generative AI, which theatre companies can deliver.[22]

Current collaborations between technology companies and performing arts collections are limited and rely on existing archives. Tech companies do not see any incentive to fund recordings of diverse, contemporary performance practices. Existing projects are limited in scope. Google's Arts & Culture section on Performing Arts,[23] for example, focuses primarily on images of theatre exhibits, sometimes enhanced with 360-degree video and machine learning-based image analysis to improve searchability and exploration of the archive. The video collection, however, is limited to rehearsal clips and short archival footage.

However, the recent research on AI LLM models can change the calculus. It indicates that 'indiscriminate use of model-generated content in training causes irreversible defects in the resulting models, in which tails of the original content distribution disappear'.[24] Simply put, when fed its own content, LLM experience 'model collapse'. That is, the AI begins to hallucinate and is unable to produce relevant content. Because of this, to be able to generate new content without experiencing model collapse, LLMs need to be constantly fed human-generated content. As a result, 'the value of data collected about genuine human interactions with systems will be increasingly valuable in the presence of LLM-generated content in data crawled from the Internet'.[25] Establishing long-term partnerships between theatres and tech companies that would digitize the historical and current performances will not only ensure that future AI models remain functional and rely on human-generated content and data sets that are current and relevant to the modern world, but will also provide access to culture that is currently denied to millions of people with disabilities, chronically ill, economically disadvantaged, and geographically distant populations, while also fairly renumerating the artists for their work.

Both theatres and tech companies should recognize the economic benefits of such partnerships. These collaborations should be supported by collective bargaining units with contracts that protect artists' rights while expanding access for people with disabilities, other marginalized populations, researchers, and similarly situated stakeholders.

## Legislation

Finally, the current international treaties adopted by the World Intellectual Property Organization (WIPO), the Beijing Treaty on Audiovisual Performances (2012),[26] and the Marrakesh VIP Treaty (formally the Marrakesh Treaty to Facilitate Access to Published Works for Persons Who Are Blind, Visually Impaired or Otherwise Print Disabled, colloquially the Marrakesh Treaty or MVT, 2013),[27] are not aligned with the latest technological developments. Article 13 of the Beijing Treaty allows for copyright exceptions, but it lacks any reference to the need for the exceptions to facilitate disability access:

> (1) Contracting Parties may, in their national legislation, provide for the same kinds of limitations or exceptions with regard to the protection of performers as they provide for, in their national legislation, in connection with the protection of copyright in literary and artistic works.

(2) Contracting Parties shall confine any limitations of or exceptions to rights provided for in this Treaty to certain special cases which do not conflict with a normal exploitation of the performance and do not unreasonably prejudice the legitimate interests of the performer.[28]

The lack of mention of disability access as a valid reason for the copyright exception once again frames disability rights as an afterthought.

The Marrakesh VIP Treaty focuses exclusively on the accessibility of printed material for the benefit of those whose disabilities make its use difficult or impossible:

> The broad definition includes persons who are blind, visually impaired, or print disabled or persons with a physical disability that prevents them from holding and manipulating a book. Works 'in the form of text, notation and/or related illustrations, whether published or otherwise made publicly available in any media', including audio books, fall within the scope of the MVT regime.[29]

Specifically, a beneficiary person is a person who:

(a) is blind;
(b) has a visual impairment or a perceptual or reading disability which cannot be improved to give visual function substantially equivalent to that of a person who has no such impairment or disability and so is unable to read printed works to substantially the same degree as a person without an impairment or disability; or
(c) is otherwise unable, through physical disability, to hold or manipulate a book or to focus or move the eyes to the extent that would be normally acceptable for reading; regardless of any other disabilities.[30]

The Marrakesh VIP Treaty includes physical disabilities only in so far as they prevent one from reading. The early version of the Marrakesh VIP Treaty 'included provisions that would have catered to other works and disabilities'.[31] Specifically, Article 15(b), which was blocked by the Obama administration at the request of the Motion Picture Association of America (MPAA), provided more flexibility as to who could benefit from the Treaty. The MPAA worried that a broad interpretation of 'visual impairment' could encompass conditions like dyslexia, potentially enabling anyone self-identifying with any disability to illegally copy and distribute copyrighted material.[32]

The most progressive and inclusive proposal was presented by the African Group; it included any persons 'suffering from visual impairment or a physical, mental, sensory, or cognitive incapacity, and persons with any other disability who, due to that disability, need an accessible format'.[33] Article 15(b) offered a similar approach:

> Contracting parties shall extend the provisions of this treaty to persons *with any other disability* who, due to that disability, need *an accessible format of a type that could be made under Article 4* to access a copyright work to substantially the same degree as a person without a disability. (emphasis mine)[34]

However, as a result of the omission of this paragraph, a large population of people with disabilities were left without any legal protection to exercise their human right to cultural access. As several legal scholars noted, 'a binding international normative framework does not exist for persons with other disabilities and for persons with visual disabilities in relation to other types of work, beyond text or print works'.[35] The objective, therefore, should be to reconcile the text of the Marrakesh VIP Treaty with the various UN declarations and conventions that assert the human right to culture and the need to remove structural and legal barriers preventing access for the people with disabilities.

The language of the Marrakesh VIP Treaty refers to the Berne Convention for its definition of what a 'work' is, with the assumption that it is fixed as 'text, notation, or illustration':

> (a) 'work' means *literary and artistic works* within the meaning of Article 2(1) of the Berne Convention for the Protection of Literary and Artistic Works, in the form of text, notation and/or related illustrations, whether published or otherwise made publicly available in any media.[36] [emphasis mine]

The Berne Convention for the Protection of Literary and Artistic *Works* (Article 2) provides the following definition of 'literary and artistic works' which

> shall include every production in the literary, scientific and artistic domain, whatever may be the mode or form of its expression, such as books, pamphlets and other writings; lectures, addresses, sermons and other works of the same nature; dramatic or dramatico-musical works; choreographic works and entertainments in dumb show; musical compositions with or without words; cinematographic works to which are assimilated works expressed by a process analogous to cinematography; works of drawing, painting, architecture, sculpture, engraving and lithography; photographic works to which are assimilated works expressed by a process analogous to photography; works of applied art; illustrations, maps, plans, sketches and three-dimensional works relative to geography, topography, architecture or science.[37]

Unlike the Convention on the Rights of Persons with Disabilities, the Marrakesh VIP Treaty does not mandate the creation of accessible materials, rather, it attempts to provide remedy once they are fixed via print publication. The Treaty's limits on formats and art forms indicate the pressing need to revisit and expand it to reflect the current developments in digital formats that facilitate an access to culture for people with disabilities. The contracting parties of both treaties must review them with the purpose of assessing to what extent the principles on which the treaties are based are extendable to newly identified problems of access, while simultaneously safeguarding balance between newly introduced exceptions and existing performers' rights.[38]

In many ways, the Marrakesh VIP Treaty can be viewed as obsolete upon arrival, not only because it excluded other disabilities and accessible formats, but also with regard to the print material for which it did make the copyright exception. The Treaty was signed in 2013, but the conversations about the need for such a treaty started much earlier. At that time, 'cross-border exchange was almost impossible and efforts were duplicated in the production of works in accessible formats'.[39] This prompted a search for a legal framework that would make it easier for countries to share their accessible collections. However, the explosion of free digital book collections available for global readership that started in the mid-2010s, and the increased availability of text-to-speech readers have made the need for the copyright exception offered by the Treaty less pressing.

Google Books launched in 2004; Google's lawsuit with The Authors Guild and the Association of American Publishers (AAP) was settled in 2008,[40] and by 2019, the collection had over 40 million books scanned in over 400 languages.[41] Open Library, which by 2011 had over one million eBooks available without restriction, launched in 2006. The Internet Archive's lending library started lending its digital books collection in 2011 with 80,000 eBooks.[42] While the Treaty allowed for self-made accessible copies of print works, it put no pressure on the publishers to provide them (leaving disabled people to fend for themselves). The technology and market pressures, however, moved at a faster pace than the laws. Today, the availability of internet libraries, eBooks, audiobooks, audio descriptions, and text-to-speech readers (now with AI-enhanced accuracy) has mostly resolved the problem of access to books not just for the visually impaired but also for the homebound, the elderly, or geographically distant readers, at least in English speaking context.[43]

MPAA's concerns about the unconstrained availability of motion pictures in digital formats, which blocked Article 15(b) of the Marrakesh VIP Treaty, have also by now been mostly resolved as the producers and copyright owners of motion picture content have made it available themselves in digital formats through a variety of streaming platforms. Netflix launched its streaming services in 2007, Amazon in 2006, and Hulu in 2008. Paramount Streaming started in 2005, and Disney took its collection online in 2019. Despite this broad availability of motion picture content (which can easily be copied and distributed), by blocking Article 15(b) of the Marrakesh VIP Treaty, the MPAA limited the copyright-exempt content to print materials. As a result, a hearing-impaired person cannot legally make a copy of a movie with captions or ASL interpreters embedded without running into copyright infringement.

In recent years, however, streaming platforms, including Netflix, Amazon, Disney+, Hulu, and YouTube have themselves added multilingual captions, and in select cases also audio descriptions to their content, implicitly recognizing that expanding the way audiences receive their content would also broaden their audience reach. Captions not only benefit hearing-impaired viewers but also language learners, non-native speakers, the elderly, and anyone else who prefers to read rather than listen. Thus, incidentally, by making their content accessible to the hearing-impaired (which the MPAA resisted during the negotiations of the Marrakesh VIP Treaty), the streaming platforms expanded the pool of people who can enjoy their offerings.[44]

Likewise, book publishers came to understand that providing audiobook format will expand their readership and, thus, increase book sales. What was initially considered a disability exception has become a standard practice with appeal to many others, as listening to audiobooks has become a common practice for busy people during other activities (riding on the train, running, exercising, and so on). These two examples of books and movies illustrate that, more often than not, expanding access for people with disabilities has unintended consequences of expanding it to other, nondisabled groups. Theatres and other performing art institutions are very much behind publishing and film industries in this regard, and should become more proactive in seeking funding and creating creative and business partnerships that would expand their reach and their own audiences. Updating both international and national legal frameworks by expanding copyright exceptions to more disabilities and more diverse content would help to accelerate this process.

In the US context, the disability laws often intentionally avoid addressing copyright issues directly, with the lawmakers assuming either that the fair use doctrine will naturally resolve potential conflicts, or that the copyright issues will be handled through contracts. Theatre presents a special challenge to this regulatory approach because digitalization for accessibility purposes creates additional copyright concerns beyond just accessibility. As a result, accessibility needs in theatre might require digital solutions that create copyright complications beyond what's typically encountered in other accessibility contexts.[45]

Moreover, in the US, and commenting on Chafee's amendment, legal scholar Blake Ellis Reid notes the need to expand Chafee's 'definition of "specialized formats" into which works could be remediated, which had previously been limited to "braille, audio, or digital text," to a more open-ended set of "accessible formats" that allows reproduction or distribution into any "alternate manner or form" that gives a print-disabled reader access to the work [and updating] definition of eligible "blind or other persons with disabilities" to whom remediated works could be distributed to a more expansive definition' that includes other disabilities.[46] Going further, the expansion of the definition of eligible accessible formats and the definition of eligible disabled persons (beyond print-related formats and disabilities) would mean including digital recordings of performing arts events as an alternative accessible format for those who are prevented by their disabilities from attending the event in person, indicating the direction in which the existing international treaties should be revised.

One could argue that any such legislation would necessarily mean that the performers are 'forced' to permit to be recorded. However, in addition to counterarguments already included earlier, there are others to consider. For one, drawing a parallel to the access provided by the Marrakesh VIP Treaty for print materials does theoretically already entail permission for an individual recording of live performance. According to the Treaty, visually impaired readers can make accessible copies for themselves or can ask someone else on their behalf (authorized proxies or institutions) to make copies of the book in any accessible format without fear of copyright breach. From this, we can infer that the physically impaired audience members who are unable to attend the live performance in person should be able to record it (or have a proxy who would do that for them) for their own personal use. This would mean that a person could sit in the audience and record the performance without the theatre's input as to the quality and the security of the future digital storage of the recording. Such an interpretation of existing laws would deprive theatres of the agency to record and make public the recordings at the level of quality, content, and exposure they find acceptable. Therefore, a proactive approach to legislation mandating accessibility through official recordings could actually provide theatres with more control over their content and its distribution, rather than less. Formal legislations would also allow theatres to seek additional funding to finance all aspects of the process.

Another argument can also be made that a group of different types of performers, mainly athletes, are already 'forced' to be recorded each time they give publicly available performance. The consent to record, in fact, is implied in the consent to perform. After all, it would be absurd for the Olympic athletes – figure skaters, or dancers for example – to request for their performance not to be recorded and transmitted on television. The permission to record is implied in the performance itself. Thus, there's a precedent for implied consent to record the public performances, and this concept could logically extend to live theatre, as it is difficult to justify exempting stage performers from arrangements that sports performers implicitly accept as part of their chosen career. Implementing such a paradigm shift in the theatre world would, however, necessitate a fundamental re-evaluation of our existing cultural assumptions about the nature of live theatre performance and the rights, and labour practices associated with them.

The ongoing pandemic-related health hazards – including the steady emergence of new immune-evasive COVID-19 variants, lack of second-generation vaccines and antivirals, and high rates of Long COVID – continue to make in-person participation in performing arts events challenging, if not impossible, for a large population. This includes the elderly, immunocompromised, Long-COVID sufferers, and the people with disabilities, adding to the already-existing excluded pre-pandemic group. Thus, the international regulatory regimes must develop a set of transnational legal guidelines and recommendations for theatres and performing artists that would enable them to seek both state and private funding for the expansion of digital access. Per the ETC report, 'Cross-European [international] legislation on this matter would assist greatly and be particularly useful for improving conditions for distribution and collaboration'.[47]

## Conclusion

In September 2024, Arts Council England, Arts Council of Northern Ireland, Arts Council of Wales, and Creative Scotland, under the umbrella of joint access scheme, All In, issued a notice that it plans to develop an industry-wide standards of accessibility. Disability-led charity Attitude is Everything[48] has been put in charge of 'developing a set of sector-wide standards for theatres, galleries, museums, libraries and other creative organisations that sign up for the scheme'.[49] The objective of the 'standards for creativity and culture, [is to] provide the sector with a baseline in excellence for meeting the needs of disabled people, covering everything from content warnings to appropriate language and expectations around physical access'.[50] Unfortunately, as of now, the projects appears to limit the concept of digital access to 'making digital communication with disabled audience more accessible, usable and inclusive'.[51] Making sure that the disabled audience members have the information about the accessibility features of the venue they plan to visit is an important consideration, however, the very notion of digital accessibility needs expansion to ensure true accessibility for those who are unable, for a variety of reasons, to travel to the performing arts venues.

Without the legal guidelines that would prioritize the needs of the disabled groups while also protecting the performers' rights, access to performing arts will continue to remain elusive for the many excluded audience members. To quote Reid further:

> It is critical for disability law to consider, particularly in an intermediated Internet ecosystem, how to allocate responsibility for the accessibility of creative works to ensure not merely that someone can, in theory, make them accessible, but indeed that someone must do so. … Disability law must consider the role of copyright holders in making their own works accessible. Where

> third-party accessibility efforts necessitate limitations and exceptions, copyright policymaking should center the interests of people with disabilities.[52]

To ensure that digital access to the performing arts is viewed as economically viable, the funding bodies, including governments and foundations, should consider international studies to determine which of the successful online and hybrid programming strategies implemented during the COVID-19 pandemic are replicable and transferable to other institutions: 'Deploying technical and creative approaches to accessibility is likely to require overcoming market failure.'[53] As Reid points out,

> Inherent in the typical instantiation of a new creative medium is the reality that copyright holders and the surrounding industry are not merely disinterested in serving people with disabilities but may not even be cognizant of the exclusionary and discriminatory effects of the medium on people who cannot access that medium on equal terms. The initial challenge for accessibility, then, is not the need to secure the permission of copyright holders to serve the market of people with disabilities, but rather to grapple in technological and creative terms with what changes are conceptually necessary to make the medium accessible.[54]

Developing a set of tools and skills that can be easily used by theatre practitioners to expand their digital programming, and thus reach previously marginalized audiences – including people with disabilities, elderly, homebound, clinically vulnerable, economically and geographically excluded, and the carers, but also diverse groups of digital natives – is the most urgent need within the performing arts ecosystem. To compete with the appeal of streaming platforms, theatres must reassess their commitment to digital programming, embracing the audiences that sustained them during the COVID lockdowns but have since been left behind. Likewise, funding bodies must include digital access as part of their regulatory and financial planning.

To quote Rufus Norris again,

> [M]aking theatre accessible is not just about reaching audiences physically; it's about removing barriers of geography, economics and age. … Throughout history, in innumerable cultures, the importance of storytelling has been secondary only to health, food, shelter and love. It is a vital part of our human need. … I look forward to a future where theatre knows no boundaries. Whether experienced in person or on screen, the magic of theatre remains a testament to the enduring power of storytelling.[55]

Recent data out of the US suggests that COVID-19 pandemic permanently altered our social habits. Survey of 34,000 participants published in the *Journal of the American Planning Association* has shown that 'the trend away from out-of-home activities and travel appears to be persisting'.[56] In fact, data indicates 'a permanent shift away from out-of-home activities and travel'.[57] The authors of the study conclude that:

> Remote work, online education, streaming video, teleshopping, Zoom parties, and the like may prove sticky, even after their public health impetus has faded. … Why is this important for planners? … A shift from out-of-home movies, theater, and sporting events in favor of streaming video and video games may weaken commercial entertainment.[58]

Although the vulnerable and marginalized groups (people with disabilities, elderly, economically and geographically excluded audience members) would be the primary beneficiaries of the increased digital access to performing arts, the organizations and institutions such as theatres, operas, and ballets, would also benefit from expanding their digital offerings, due to the permanent changes in audience habits and expectations.

> Moreover, for theatre workers and artists, international cultural mobility is a vital aspect of a professional career, not merely for the cultural and intellectual enrichment it fosters, but also for the economic stability it can provide. The international dimension is especially crucial for artists and cultural practitioners whose local or national ecosystems fail to offer such opportunities.[59]

Digital presence, including cross-border and transnational streaming, and other online initiatives, are powerful triggers for international cultural mobility, including network building, dissemination of knowledge, and transcultural collaborations. Theatres and other performing arts institutions must recognize the mutual benefit of greater digital access and bring back and expand the programming which many of them developed during the COVID-19 lockdowns.

As increased digitalization and AI become more prominent in our debates around copyright laws, human right to culture for people with disabilities and other marginalized groups must be part of that conversation. Although greater digital access to culture won't solve all of the needs – many communities don't have sufficiently advanced internet access to be able to stream shows – it is the first step in creating more equal and socially coherent societies. To quote Javaad Alipoor:

> Internet culture has changed how art works. The gap between community and professional practice, audience development and performance, critic and fan has become much closer. Right now, when we ask more than ever what theatre can do to address historic injustice, support communities and transform the relationship between

> the central and the supposedly 'peripheral', this is the answer: in its own way, a genuinely contemporary theatre must do the same.[60]

In June 2025, Rachel Zegler, who has been staring as Evita, sang *Don't Cry for Me, Argentina* from an external balcony at the London Palladium. The event was livestreamed back to the audience in the theatre, a directorial choice which attracted much media attention. Since it repeated every evening around 9 pm, the outside audiences have started growing, prompting Lyn Gardner to comment:

> the most interesting aspect of the coverage is the way it unwittingly exposes some of the uneasy tensions in theatre around space and access. ... As has often been the case in theatre when new technologies have arrived – whether they are ways of moving the scenery at the press of a button or using microphones – there is a rumbling fear that somehow the essential magic will be lost. ... Zegler on the Palladium balcony could be the cultural moment when the live stream goes mainstream and becomes more accepted as a useful tool, one that (as the media interest unwittingly reveals) also sheds a light on what theatre is and who gets to see it.[61]

# Notes

## one Introduction

1 Special thanks to Doug Reside for contributing his insights to this section.
2 Special thanks to Jessica Rizzo for bringing this article to my attention.
3 Reid, 2021, 2173.
4 United Nations, 1948, np.
5 United Nations, 1966a, np.
6 United Nations, 1966b, np.
7 United Nations, 2007, np.
8 Special thanks to Richard Misek for contributing his insights to this section.
9 See, for example, National Academies of Sciences, Engineering, and Medicine, 2020; Vasan et al, 2023; and Smith et al, 2020.
10 Floch, 2024, 3.
11 Council of the European Union, 2024, § 7.
12 Council of the European Union, 2024, § 11.
13 Council of the European Union, 2024, § 13 & 14.
14 United Nations Department of Economic and Social Affairs, nd, np.
15 WHO, 2018, np.
16 Ncube et al, 2020, 154.
17 metaLAB(at) Harvard, 2021.
18 metaLAB(at) Harvard, 2021.
19 Future Stage Research Group, 2021.
20 metaLAB(at) Harvard, 2021.

## two Theatre and Digitality

1 Teachout, 2013.
2 Romanska, 2014, 10.
3 Silber and Triplett, 2015.
4 Ostrower and the Wallace Foundation, 2024.
5 Lewis, 2014. For the full press release and programme of the exhibit, see Barbican, 2018.
6 Special thanks to Ariel Sibert and Ashley Chang for suggesting some of these examples.
7 Todorut, 2016.
8 Beeching, 2017, np.

[9] See chapters Eckersall et al; McNeilly; Todorut; Dean; Thomas; and Zuckerberg, in Romanska (2014).
[10] *Theater: Digital Feelings*, 2016.
[11] *Theater: Digital Dramaturgies*, 2012.
[12] Yakubovskaya, 2019.
[13] Tompkins, 2023, np.
[14] European Commission, 2019, 9.
[15] Societies and Cultures Institute, 2024, 16.
[16] Societies and Cultures Institute, 2024, 2.
[17] Societies and Cultures Institute, 2024, 2.
[18] Romanska, 2021.
[19] Societies and Cultures Institute, 2024, 20.
[20] Societies and Cultures Institute, 2024, 14–16.
[21] Loeppky, 2021.
[22] Brownlow-Calkin, 2021, np.
[23] Jackson and National Endowment for the Arts, 2023.
[24] National Endowment for the Arts, 2023.
[25] National Endowment for the Arts, 2023, 2.
[26] National Endowment for the Arts, 2023, 2–4.
[27] National Endowment for the Arts, 2023, 6.
[28] National Endowment for the Arts, 2023, 1.
[29] National Endowment for the Arts, 2023, 2.
[30] National Endowment for the Arts, 2023, 3.
[31] National Endowment for the Arts, 2023.
[32] National Endowment for the Arts, 2023, 5.
[33] National Endowment for the Arts, 2023, 7.
[34] National Endowment for the Arts, 2023.
[35] National Endowment for the Arts, 2023.
[36] Misek et al, 2022.
[37] Misek et al, 52.
[38] Misek et al, 40.
[39] Misek et al, 59.
[40] Misek et al, 40.
[41] Misek et al, 36.
[42] Misek et al, 61.
[43] Klich and Rowson, 2022, 53.
[44] Klich and Rowson, 2022, 53.
[45] Klich and Rowson, 2022, 53.
[46] Klich and Rowson, 2022, 6.
[47] Hawthorne and European Theatre Convention, 2023.
[48] Hawthorne and European Theatre Convention, 2023, 23.
[49] Hawthorne and European Theatre Convention, 2023, 23.

50 Hawthorne and European Theatre Convention, 2023, 37.
51 Special thanks to Heidi Wiley and Christy Romer for sharing the ETC report.
52 Hawthorne and European Theatre Convention, 2023, 37.
53 Hawthorne and European Theatre Convention, 2023, 37.
54 Creative Australia, 2023a.
55 Creative Australia, 2023a, 2.
56 Creative Australia, 2023a, 3.
57 Masso, 2020, np.
58 Masso, 2020, np.
59 Iskander, 2020, np.
60 Smith, 2024, np.
61 On The Move, 2021, 4.
62 On The Move, 2021, 10.
63 On The Move, 2021, 71.
64 Societies and Cultures Institute, 2024, 18.
65 Misek et al, 2022, 45.
66 Luckhurst, 2024b, np.
67 Klich and Rowson, 2022, 41.
68 Chambers, 2025c, np.
69 Akbar, 2024.
70 Parker, 2024, np.
71 Thorpe, 2023, np.
72 Luckhurst, 2024a, np.
73 Special thanks to David Ball and Richard Misek for contributing their insights to this section.
74 Luckhurst, 2024c, np.
75 Indigo Ltd, 2025, np.
76 Indigo Ltd, 2025, np.
77 Indigo Ltd, 2025, np.
78 Chambers, 2025b, np.
79 Chambers, 2025a, np.
80 Ernst and Young, 2021.
81 European Commission, Directorate-General for Education, Youth, Sport and Culture, 2022, 6–7.
82 European Commission, Directorate-General for Education, Youth, Sport and Culture, 2022, 41.
83 European Commission, Directorate-General for Education, Youth, Sport and Culture, 2022, 88.
84 European Commission, Directorate-General for Education, Youth, Sport and Culture, 2022, 31.
85 European Commission, Directorate-General for Education, Youth, Sport and Culture, 2022, 88.

86 European Commission, Directorate-General for Education, Youth, Sport and Culture, 2022, 56.
87 de Brogniez and Vandenbulke, 2022.
88 de Brogniez and Vandenbulke, 2022, 7.
89 Marshall, 2024, np.
90 Paulson and Hernández, 2022, np.
91 Goldstein, 2022, np.
92 Hall, 2022, np.
93 Paulson and Hernández, 2022, np.
94 Sperling, 2024, np.
95 Brancaccio and Dang, 2022, np.
96 Gelt, 2022, np.
97 Willman, 2023, np.
98 Willman, 2023, np.
99 Vaughan, 2023, np.
100 Stevens, 2023, np.
101 Paulson and Hernández, 2022, np.
102 Broadway League, 2025, 3, 5, 8.
103 Shaw, 2025.
104 Ritter, 2025, np.
105 Ritter, 2025, np.
106 Bohra and Lu, 2023, np.
107 Green, 2024, np.
108 Ruhl, 2024.
109 Commonwealth of Australia, 2021.
110 Commonwealth of Australia, 2021, 69–71.
111 Commonwealth of Australia, 2021, 6 (submission #344).
112 Commonwealth of Australia, 2021, 107–109.
113 Commonwealth of Australia, 2021, 107–109.
114 Peach, 2022, np.
115 Peach, 2022, np.
116 Creative Australia, 2023b, np.
117 Creative Australia, 2023b, np.
118 Creative Australia, 2023b, np.

## three Successful Case Studies

1 Societies and Cultures Institute, 2024, 13–16.
2 Fierberg, 2023.
3 https://www.lolst.org/ [Accessed 30 May 2024].
4 Special thanks to Jim Augustine for sharing the story and data of LOLSTR.

5 Vincentelli, 2021.

6 Special thanks to the ARLEKIN! and Sarah Stackhouse for providing their production history and data.

7 Compare Trueman, 2013. The exact numbers of participating cinemas fluctuate with each specific broadcast.

8 Cavendish, 2013, np.

9 Peters, 2014, 124–125.

10 Cf http://ntlive.nationaltheatre.org.uk/about-us [Accessed 12 November 2013].

11 NESTA, 2011, 19, 38.

12 NESTA, 2011, 23.

13 Peters, 2014, 124–125.

14 Norris, 2024, np.

15 Misek et al, 2022.

16 Blurb posted on the company Darkfield's website, https://www.darkfield.org/paradise [Accessed 24 April 2024].

17 Misek et al, 2022, 27.

18 Misek et al, 2022, 27.

19 Misek et al, 2022, 28.

20 Misek et al, 2022, 39.

21 Misek et al, 2022, 39.

22 Katie Hawthorne and European Theatre Convention (2023, May), *Digital Theatre – Digital Strategies and Business Models in European Theatre*, https://rb.gy/fgwzo6 [Accessed 7 April 2024]. This subchapter summarizes and reflects on the case studies and information contained in the ETC report.

23 Hawthorne and European Theatre Convention, 2023, 51.

24 Hawthorne and European Theatre Convention, 2023, 49.

25 Palatnyi, quoted in Hawthorne and European Theatre Convention, 2023.

26 Palatnyi, quoted in Hawthorne and European Theatre Convention, 2023, 55.

27 https://operavision.eu/ [Accessed 9 November 2025].

28 https://ninateka.pl/ [Accessed 9 November 2025].

29 https://madelen.ina.fr/ [Accessed 9 November 2025].

30 https://www.prospero-theatre.tv/ [Accessed 9 November 2025].

31 https://www.marquee.tv/ [Accessed 9 November 2025].

32 https://www.dramox.tv/ [Accessed 9 November 2025].

33 https://www.broadwayhd.com/ [Accessed 9 November 2025].

34 https://www.scenesaver.co.uk/-is [Accessed 9 November 2025].

35 https://www.digitaltheatre.com/ [Accessed 9 November 2025].

36 https://www.digitaltheatreplus.com/ [Accessed 9 November 2025].

37 Special thanks to David Ball from DT+ for sharing the information about their platform.

38 https://thetheatretimes.com/iotfestival/ [Accessed 9 November 2025].

39 Romanska and Lech, 2024.

## four Real and Perceived Challenges

1 Societies and Cultures Institute, 2024, 16.

2 Hawthorne and European Theatre Convention, 2023, 45.

3 Comley, 2023.

4 Misek et al, 2022, 52.

5 Leguina et al, 2023.

6 Norris, 2024, np.

7 Norris, 2024, np.

8 See article 11 of the 1886 Berne Convention for the Protection of Literary and Artistic Works and article 8 of the 1996 World Copyright Treaty, https://www.wipo.int/wipolex/en/text/283698 [Accessed 24 August 2024].

9 See article 7(1)2 of the 1962 Rome Convention for the protection of performers, producers of phonograms and broadcasting organizations and article 6(ii) of the 2012 Beijing Treaty on audiovisual performances.

10 See articles 10 and 11 of the 2012 Beijing Treaty on audiovisual performances.

11 See article 15(1)b of the 1961 Rome Convention and article 2*bis*(2) of the 1886 Berne Convention.

12 Directive 2001/29/EC of the European Parliament and of the Council of 22 May 2001 on the harmonization of certain aspects of copyright and related rights in the information society, https://eur-lex.europa.eu/eli/dir/2001/29/oj [Accessed 24 August 2024].

13 Directive (EU) 2019/790 of the European Parliament and of the Council of 17 April 2019 on copyright and related rights in the Digital Single Market and amending Directives 96/9/EC and 2001/29/EC, https://eur-lex.europa.eu/eli/dir/2019/790/oj [Accessed 24 August 2024].

14 Directive (EU) 2019/790 of the European Parliament and of the Council of 17 April 2019 on copyright and related rights in the Digital Single Market and amending Directives 96/9/EC and 2001/29/EC. Art. 18(1) and Recital (73) of Directive 2019/790.

15 These types of provisions could already be found in national laws. For example, French law imposes an obligation of a remuneration that is *proportional* to the receipts from the use of the work in the case of assignment of such a right (Art. L. 131-4(1) of the French Code of Intellectual Property) – the assignment may nonetheless be free of charge (Art. L122-7 of the same code). Following the transposition of the Directive 2019/790, Belgian Law now contains similar provisions (see Art. XI.167/1 and XI.205/1 of the Belgian Code of Economic Law).

16 Special thanks to Ioan Kaes for his insights on the laws and for helping me grapple with these arguments.
17 Loeppky, 2021, np.
18 Loeppky, 2021, np.
19 Loeppky, 2021, np.
20 National Endowment for the Arts Office of Accessibility, 2010.
21 ADA.gov, 2010, np.
22 UK Government, 2010.
23 Special thanks to Richard Misek for his insights to this section.
24 UK Government, 2023.
25 UK Government, 2023.
26 European Union Agency for Fundamental Rights, nd.
27 European Parliament, 2018.
28 As a reminder, a directive is an EU legal act that applies to Member States, which are responsible for implementing those measures (in contrast to regulations, which are directly applicable to Member States' internal orders).
29 European Parliament, 2010.
30 European Parliament, 2018.
31 Australian Human Rights Commission, 1992, np.
32 Live Performance Australia Guide, 2011, np.
33 'The Chafee Amendment: 17 United States SC. 121 & 121A', 1996.
34 See *Authors Guild, Inc. v. HathiTrust*, 2014.
35 United States, 118th Congress, 2nd Session, 2024.
36 United States, 118th Congress, 2nd Session, 2024, np.
37 World Intellectual Property Organization (WIPO), 2013.
38 United Kingdom, 2014.
39 United Kingdom Intellectual Property Office, 2014/2021, np.
40 United Kingdom Intellectual Property Office, 2014/2021, np.
41 United Kingdom Intellectual Property Office, 2014/2021, np.
42 See Schechner, 1977; 1985.
43 United Kingdom, 2014, np.
44 Special thanks to Ioan Kaes for his insights on this subject.
45 Special thanks to Ioan Kaes for his insights on the nature of these laws.
46 de Brogniez and Vandenbulke, 2022.
47 In addition to the study, these issues are also addressed in de Brogniez and Vandenbulke (2023).
48 See Art. 7 of the Rome Convention for the Protection of Performers, Producers of Phonograms and Broadcasting Organizations of October 16th, 1961 (hereafter 'Rome Convention').
49 Many States – as is the case in Belgian law – have established a presumption of assignment of related rights in favour of producers of audiovisual

works. Such a presumption has been judged compatible with European Law by the Court of Justice, since the latter can be rebutted (CJEU, 9 February 2012, Martin Luksan v. Petrus van der Let, case C-277/10, ECLI:EU:C:2012:65). However, the issue remains: what is an 'audiovisual work' and, more precisely: is the mere recording of a play an audiovisual work which is distinct from the play? This question is settled at the national level. For example, the Brussels Court of Appeal has ruled that, for a recording to constitute an audiovisual work allowing this presumption, it is required that the recording itself be a work distinct from the work recorded, that it is, in itself, original (see Brussels, 7 May 2021, confirmed by Cass. be., 29 April 2022, *A&M*, 2021/4, pp 496 *et seq*., note. M. de Brogniez and A. Vandenbulke).

50 Due to a lack of knowledge of the legislation, many operators mistakenly believe that a single payment for the use of a work to a rights management society leads to authorization for all modes of exploitation.

51 Directive (EU) 2019/790 of the European Parliament and of the Council of 17 April 2019 on copyright and related rights in the Digital Single Market and amending Directives 96/9/EC and 2001/29/EC, O.J. E.U, L.130/29, 17 May 2019 (hereafter 'Directive 2019/790'), https://eur-lex.europa.eu/eli/dir/2019/790/oj [Accessed 19 March 2024].

52 Art. 18(1) and Recital (73) of Directive 2019/790.

53 These types of provisions could already be found in national laws. For example, French law imposes an obligation of a remuneration that is proportional to the receipts from the use of the work in the case of assignment of such a right (Art. L. 131-4(1) of the French Code of Intellectual Property) – the assignment may nonetheless be free of charge (Art. L122-7 of the same code). Following the transposition of the Directive 2019/790, Belgian Law now contains similar provisions (see Art. XI.167/1 and XI.205/1 of the Belgian Code of Economic Law).

54 Recital (82) of Directive 2019/790. We think that there is nothing to exclude assigning the right free of charge, as it is explicitly provided in some national laws.

55 European Union Parliament, 2001.

56 'It is in any case important for the Member States to adopt all necessary measures to facilitate access to works by persons suffering from a disability which constitutes an obstacle to the use of the works themselves, and to pay particular attention to accessible formats.'

57 European Parliament, 2017a. This Directive is supplemented by European Parliament (2017b).

58 Art. 3(1)(b) of the Directive.

59 Romanska, 2012, 5.

60 Szulczynski, 1996, 499.

61 Tymicki and Niezgoda, 1986, 22.

62 Teatr Polskiej Telewizji, https://teatrtv.vod.tvp.pl/ [Accessed 5 April 2024].

63 The numbers are from the reports by Poland's National Broadcasting Agency: https://www.gov.pl/web/krrit/ogromny-spadek-ogladalnosci-serwisu-informacyjnego-tvp-1930-raport-z-monitoringu-krrit [Accessed 30 May 2024]; and Poland's National News Agency: https://www.pap.pl/aktualnosci/sukces-teatru-telewizji-musical-1989-inspirowany-hamiltonem-z-rekordowa-ogladalnoscia [Accessed 30 May 2024].

64 https://ninateka.pl/vod/teatr/ [Accessed 9 November 2025].

65 Krajewski and Frąckowiak, 2021, 20–22; and Kalinowska et al, 2021, 40–44.

66 Buchner et al, 2021, 13, 28–30, 60, 63.

67 Lech, 2020.

68 Buchner et al, 2021, 23–30, 71–80; Ćwikła et al, 2021, 107–108; and Krajewski and Frąckowiak, 2021, 15–25, 45–47, 52–54.

69 Buchner et al, 2021, 24–27, 30, 58.

70 Kietlińska, 2021, 21–28.

71 Buchner et al, 2021, 24–27, 30, 58; Kalinowska et al, 2021, 43–49, 125–126; and Ilczuk et al, 2021, 5–9, 31–34.

72 Ilczuk et al, 2021, 37.

73 Poland was the last of 27 EU member states to implement these directives. On 26 July 2024, the SEJM approved a set of additional amendments agreed upon by the Senate and thereby passed the long-awaited law on copyright and related rights.

74 Royalties for music works can be negotiated by the collecting management agencies or independent management agencies or directly by the artist. The choice is made by artist. Infor, 2024, np.

75 'Ustawa z dnia 26 lipca 2024 r. o zmianie ustawy o prawie autorskim i prawach pokrewnych, ustawy o ochronie baz danych oraz ustawy o zbiorowym zarządzaniu prawami autorskimi i prawami pokrewnymi', Dziennik Ustaw 1254 (2024) https://isap.sejm.gov.pl/isap.nsf/DocDetails.xsp?id=WDU20240001254 [Accessed 19 June 2025].

76 Others include ZAiKS (Society of Authors and Stage Composers); ZPAV (Union of Audio-Video Producers); STOART (The Union of Performing Artists); and SAWP (Society of the Performing Artists of Musical and Verbal-Musical Works).

77 ZASP, 2023.

78 ZASP, 2023.

79 Commonwealth of Australia, 2021, 137–139.

80 Commonwealth of Australia, 2021, 34. Professor David Throsby, Dr Jan Zwar, and Dr Paul Crosby, Submission 338, p 5 [Accessed 13 February 2024].
81 Australian Libraries and Archives Copyright Coalition, nd.
82 See Australian Government, 2018.
83 Australian Libraries and Archives Copyright Coalition, 2023, 7–8.
84 WIPO, 2022.
85 Harpur, 2017.
86 Harpur, Stein, and Ncube, 2023.
87 Harpur and Stein, 2021.
88 Harpur and Stein, 2021.
89 Reid, 2021, 2174.
90 Reid, 2021, 2174.
91 Johnson, 2010, 181, 186.
92 Reid, 2021, 2176.

## five Recommendations

1 Orland, 2024, np.
2 Copyright.gov, 2024, 11, l. 10.
3 Copyright.gov, 2024, 25, ll. 23–24.
4 Salvador, 2024, np.
5 US Copyright Office, 2024, 8.
6 US Copyright Office, 2024, 29.
7 Knibbs, 2024, np.
8 https://nlsbard.loc.gov/nlsbardprod/login/NLS [Accessed 9 November 2025].
9 National Library Service for the Blind and Print Disabled, nd-a.
10 National Library Service for the Blind and Print Disabled, nd-b, np.
11 https://madelen.ina.fr/ [Accessed 9 November 2025].
12 https://ninateka.pl/ [Accessed 9 November 2025].
13 Okundaye, 2024, np.
14 Taylor, 2003. Also see Borggreen and Gade, 2013.
15 Mahari, Fjeld, and Epstein, 2023.
16 Felicetty, 2024.
17 United States Copyright Office, 2025, iii.
18 United States Copyright Office, 2025, 38.
19 United States Copyright Office, 2025, 41.
20 Knibbs, 2025.
21 Schrader, 2025.
22 See Laney, 2025.
23 https://artsandculture.google.com/project/performing-arts [Accessed 9 November 2025].

[24] Shumailov et al, 2024, np.
[25] Shumailov et al, 2024, np.
[26] World Intellectual Property Organization (WIPO), 2012, 9.
[27] World Intellectual Property Organization (WIPO), 2013a.
[28] World Intellectual Property Organization (WIPO), 2012, 9.
[29] World Intellectual Property Organization (WIPO), 2013b, np.
[30] World Intellectual Property Organization (WIPO), 2013a, np.
[31] Ncube et al, 2020, np.
[32] Bezbozhna, 2014, 20. Also see Ecology International, 2013.
[33] Bezbozhna, 2014, 19.
[34] Bezbozhna, 2014, 19.
[35] Bezbozhna, 2014, 19.
[36] World Intellectual Property Organization (WIPO), 2013a, np.
[37] Berne Convention for the Protection of Literary and Artistic Works (as amended on 28 September 1979).
[38] Special thanks to Ioan Kaes for his insights on this topic.
[39] Bezbozhna, 2014, 16.
[40] Google Press Center, 2008, np.
[41] Lee, 2019.
[42] Kaplan, 2011.
[43] The availability of print and motion picture content is dominated by the English language, which makes it difficult for disabled non-English speakers to access. In recent years, disability groups have been advocating for the languages developed in response to disabilities (Braille, ASL) to be recognized as full languages, with their own distinct cultures. Translations into these languages would then be treated like any other translations (special thanks to Kasia Lech for this note, private correspondence, 19 October 2024).
[44] In addition to captions, by 2022, Netflix supported over 11,000 hours of audio-description in more than 30 languages. See Spangler, 2022, np. As of 2024, Disney+ offers audio description for most of its content. See Disney+ https://help.disneyplus.com/article/disneyplus-en-us-audio-description [Accessed 21 October 2024]. OpenAI's DALL-E and other LLMs like ChatGPT or Claude.ai can generate image descriptions and alt text, potentially improving accessibility for visually impaired participants across various platforms.
[45] Special thanks to Blake Ellis Reid for this note.
[46] Reid, 2021, 2203–2204.
[47] Hawthorne and European Theatre Convention, 2023, np.
[48] https://attitudeiseverything.org.uk/industry/all-of-our-resources/ [Accessed 10 January 2025].
[49] Hemley, 2024, np.

50 Hemley, 2024, np.
51 Hemley, 2024, np.
52 Reid, 2021, 2222–2223.
53 Reid, 2021, 2173.
54 Reid, 2021, 2172.
55 Norris, 2024, np.
56 Morris, Speroni, and Taylor, 2024, 361.
57 Morris, Speroni, and Taylor, 2024, 361.
58 Morris, Speroni, and Taylor, 2024, 362.
59 Floch, 2024, 3.
60 Alipoor, 2020, np.
61 Gardner, 2025, np.

# References


ADA.gov (2010, September) '2010 ADA Standards for Accessible Design', https://www.ada.gov/law-and-regs/design-standards/2010-stds/ [Accessed 13 February 2024].

Akbar, Arifa (2024) 'Theatre Needs Risk-Takers Like Kwame Kwei-Armah Whose Young Vic Has Been Dynamite', *The Guardian*, 8 February, https://www.theguardian.com/stage/2024/feb/08/theatre-needs-risk-takers-like-kwame-kwei-armah-whose-young-vic-has-been-dynamite [Accessed 5 April 2024].

Alipoor, Javaad (2020) 'Theatre Theatre 2021: Javaad Alipoor on … Digital Theatre', *The Stage*, 24 June, https://www.thestage.co.uk/features/theatre-2021-javaad-alipoor-on-digital-theatre [Accessed 22 June 2025].

Australian Government (2018) Copyright Amendment (Service Providers) Act 2018, (Cth), https://www.legislation.gov.au/Details/C2018A00071 [Accessed 13 February 2024].

Australian Human Rights Commission (1992) 'Disability Discrimination', https://humanrights.gov.au/our-work/disability-rights/disability-discrimination [Accessed 13 February 2024].

Australian Libraries and Archives Copyright Coalition (nd) 'Advocacy', https://alacc.org.au/advocacy/ [Accessed 13 February 2024].

Australian Libraries and Archives Copyright Coalition (2023) *Joint Submission in Response to the Copyright Enforcement Review 2022–2023*, pp 7–8, https://alacc.org.au/joint-submission-in-response-to-the-copyright-enforcement-review-2022-2023/ [Accessed 16 February 2024].

*Authors Guild, Inc. v. HathiTrust*, 755 F.3d 87 (2d Cir. 2014), https://www.copyright.gov/fair-use/summaries/authorsguild-hathitrust-2dcir2014.pdf [Accessed 28 April 2024].

Barbican (2018) 'Barbican's "Digital Revolution" Celebrates Computing Creativity at WF CENTRAL Beijing', https://www.wfcentral.cn/en/uploadfile/2018/0207/20180207074148253.pdf [Accessed 4 February 2024].

Beeching, Alexander (2017) 'Open Online Theatre Invites Its Audience to "Walk into Space"', *The Theatre Times*, 11 January, https://thetheatretimes.com/open-online-theatre-invites-audience-walk-space/ [Accessed 4 February 2024].

Berne Convention for the Protection of Literary and Artistic Works (as amended on 28 September 1979) (1979) https://www.wipo.int/wipolex/en/text/283698 [Accessed 14 November 2024].

Bezbozhna, Olga (2014) *The Marrakesh Treaty for Persons with Visual Impairments: The Intersection Between Copyright and Human Rights Knowledge*, Lund University, https://lup.lub.lu.se/luur/download?func=downloadFile&recordOId=4388852&fileOId=4388872 [Accessed 28 July 2024].

Bohra, Neelam and Lu, Wendy (2023) 'As Presenters Cut Back on Streams, Some Disabled Arts Lovers Feel Left Out', *New York Times*, 14 April, https://www.nytimes.com/2023/04/14/arts/disabled-people-streaming-performances.html [Accessed 7 February 2024].

Borggreen, Gunhild, and Gade, Rune (eds) (2013) *Performing Archives / Archives of Performance*, Museum Tusculanum Press.

Brancaccio, David, and Dang, Jarrett (2022) 'Theaters Are Still Trying to Regain Their Pre-pandemic Footing', *Marketplace*, 6 October, https://www.marketplace.org/2022/10/06/theaters-are-still-trying-to-regain-their-pre-pandemic-footing/ [Accessed 7 February 2024].

Broadway League (2025, February) *The Demographics of the Broadway Audience 2023–2024*. The Broadway League, https://www.broadwayleague.com/research/research-reports [Accessed 7 February 2025].

Brownlow-Calkin, Rosie (2021) 'The Jury Is in on Virtual Theatre', *American Theatre*, 8 November, https://www.americantheatre.org/2021/11/08/the-jury-is-in-on-virtual-theatre/ [Accessed 4 February 2024].

Buchner, Anna, Fereniec-Błońska, Katarzyna, Kalinowska, Katarzyna, and Wierzbicka, Maria (2021) *Obecność teatrów w przestrzeni online w trakcie pandemii*, Instytut Teatralny, https://www.instytut-teatralny.pl/wp-content/uploads/2021/03/obecnosc-teatrow-w-przestrzeni-online-w-trakcie-pandemii.pdf [Accessed 9 November 2025].

Cavendish, Dominic (2013) 'Should Live Theatre Be Shown in Cinema?', *The Telegraph*, 30 October.

'The Chafee Amendment: 17 United States SC. 121 & 121A' (1996) Library of Congress, https://www.loc.gov/nls/who-we-are/laws-regulations/copyright-law-amendment-1996-pl-104-197/#:~:text=The%20amendment%20allows%20authorized%20entities,use%20by%20print%2Ddisabled%20persons [Accessed 24 April 2024].

Chambers, Katie (2025a) 'Theatre Leaders Contemplate "Virtual Understudies" at SOLT and UK Theatre Panel', *The Stage*, 25 May, https://www.thestage.co.uk/news/news/theatre-leaders-contemplate-virtual-understudies-at-solt-and-uk-theatre-panel [Accessed 8 June 2025].

Chambers, Katie (2025b) 'UK's Creative Industries "Falling Behind" Amid Tech Expansion, Report Claims', *The Stage*, 14 April, https://www.thestage.co.uk/news/uks-creative-industries-falling-behind-amid-tech-expansion-report-claims [Accessed 26 April 2025].

Chambers, Katie (2025c) '"Unsustainable": A Third of Theatres Will Post a Deficit This Year – Report', *The Stage*, 22 May, https://www.thestage.co.uk/news/unsustainable-a-third-of-theatres-will-report-a-deficit-this-year-report? [Accessed 8 June 2025].

Comley, Bonnie (2023) 'Why Aren't There More Digital Captures of Broadway Shows?' *BroadwayWorld.com*, 14 March, https://www.broadwayworld.com/article/-Why-Arent-There-More-Digital-Captures-of-Broadway-Shows-20230314 [Accessed 4 February 2024].

Commonwealth of Australia (2021) *Sculpting a National Cultural Plan: Igniting a Post-COVID Economy for the Arts*, https://www.aph.gov.au/Parliamentary_Business/Committees/House/Communications/Arts/Report [Accessed 7 February 2024].

Copyright.gov (2024) 'Transcript of Proceedings in the Matter of Section 1201 Public Hearing Proposed Class 6(b) Video Games – Preservation and Proposed Class 6(a) Computer Programs Preservation', https://www.copyright.gov/1201/2024/hearing-transcripts/240418-Section-1201-Public-Hearing-Class6a-6b.pdf page 11, line 10 [Accessed 30 May 2024].

Council of the European Union (2024) 'Council Conclusions on Improving and Fostering Access to Culture', *Official Journal of the European Union*, C/2024/7446, § 7, § 11, § 13, § 14, https://eur-lex.europa.eu/legal-content/EN/TXT/HTML/?uri=OJ:C_202407446 [Accessed 4 January 2025].

Creative Australia (2023a) 'Creating Value: Results of the National Arts Participation Survey', 19 September, https://creative.gov.au/advocacy-and-research/creating-value/ [Accessed 5 February 2024].

Creative Australia (2023b) 'The Digital Front Row: Understanding Online and Digital Theatre Audiences', https://creative.gov.au/advocacy-and-research/the-digital-front-row-understanding-online-and-digital-theatre-audiences/ [Accessed 11 January 2025].

Ćwikła, Małgorzata, Laberscheck, Marcin, Rapior, Waldemar, and Smolarska Zofia (2021) *Krytyka teatralna w Polsce w czasie pandemii Covid-19*, Instytut Teatralny, https://www.instytut-teatralny.pl/wp-content/uploads/2021/04/instytut-teatralny-raport-krytyka-teatralna-w-polsce-w-czasie-pandemii-covid-19.pdf [Accessed 9 November 2025].

de Brogniez, Maxime, and Vandenbulke, Antoine (2022) 'Performing Arts Recordings and Broadcasts – A Practical Manual on Author's and Related Rights', https://www.europeantheatre.eu/download-attached/b0Q1kNJ8g4PmMJOrMGOIptmj0makskFDkzLAwwbNnFwdfLLAYq [Accessed 6 February 2024].

de Brogniez, Maxime and Vandenbulke, Antoine (2023) 'The Audiovisual Broadcast of Performing Arts: From the Stage to the Screen – Legal Issues', *International Journal for the Semiotics of Law* 36, 1971–90, https://link.springer.com/article/10.1007/s11196-023-09983-0 [Accessed 16 March 2024].

Eckersall, Peter, Grehan, Helena, and Scheer, Edward (2014) 'New Media Dramaturgy', in Magda Romanska (ed) *The Routledge Companion to Dramaturgy*, Routledge, pp 375–80.

Ecology International (June 2013) 'Briefing Materials: "The Evolution of Treaty Beneficiaries: Marrakesh Note 1"', https://www.keionline.org/r2r/marrakesh [Accessed 20 October 2024].

Ellis Reid, Blake (2021) 'Copyright and Disability', *California Law Review* 109(19–16): 2173–223, https://www.californialawreview.org/print/copyright-and-disability [Accessed 25 April 2024].

Ernst and Young (2021, January) 'Rebuilding Europe: The Cultural and Creative Economy Before and After the COVID-19 Crisis', https://assets.ey.com/content/dam/ey-sites/ey-com/fr_fr/topics/government-and-public-sector/panorama-europeen-des-industries-culturelles-et-creatives/ey-panorama-des-icc-2021.pdf?download [Accessed 6 February 2024].

European Commission (2019) 'Manifesto Culture for the Future', *Culture Exchange*, https://www.acp-ue-culture.eu/en/blog/the-manifesto-culture-for-the-future-is-out/ [Accessed 8 June 2024].

European Commission, Directorate-General for Education, Youth, Sport and Culture (2022) *Study 'The Situation of Theatres in the EU Member States' – Executive Summary*, Publications Office of the European Union, https://data.europa.eu/doi/10.2766/43674 [Accessed 6 February 2024].

European Parliament and Council of the EU (2010) *Directive 2010/13/EU of the European Parliament and of the Council*, https://eur-lex.europa.eu/legal-content/EN/TXT/HTML/?uri=CELEX:02010L0013-20181218 [Accessed 8 March 2024].

European Parliament and Council of the EU (2017a) 'Directive (EU) 2017/1564 of the European Parliament and of the Council of 13 September 2017 on certain permitted uses of certain works and other subject matter protected by copyright and related rights for the benefit of persons who are blind, visually impaired or otherwise print-disabled and amending Directive 2001/29/EC on the harmonisation of certain aspects of copyright and related rights in the information society', https://eur-lex.europa.eu/legal-content/EN/TXT/?uri=CELEX:32017L1564 [Accessed 8 October 2024].

European Parliament and Council of the EU (2017b) 'Regulation (EU) 2017/1563 of the European Parliament and of the Council of 13 September 2017 on the cross-border exchange between the Union and third countries of accessible format copies of certain works and other subject matter protected by copyright and related rights for the benefit of persons who are blind, visually impaired or otherwise print-disabled', https://eur-lex.europa.eu/legal-content/EN/TXT/?uri=celex%3A32017R1563 [Accessed 8 October 2024].

European Parliament and Council of the EU (2018) 'Directive (EU) 2018/1808 of the European Parliament and of the Council of 14 November 2018', https://eur-lex.europa.eu/legal-content/EN/TXT/PDF/?uri=CELEX:32018L1808&rid=9 [Accessed 19 March 2024].

European Union Agency for Fundamental Rights (nd) 'People with Disabilities', https://fra.europa.eu/en/theme/people-disabilities#:~:text=The%20EU's%20Charter%20of%20Fundamental,the%20life%20of%20the%20community [Accessed 13 February 2024].

European Union Parliament (2001) 'Directive 2001/29/EC of the European Parliament and of the Council of 22 May 2001 on the Harmonisation of Certain Aspects of Copyright and Related Rights in the Information Society', https://eur-lex.europa.eu/legal-content/EN/TXT/HTML/?uri=CELEX:32001L0029 [Accessed 8 March 2024].

Felicetty, Jacob (2024, May 10) 'Windows into the Future: New Horizons & Implications for the Copyrightability of AI-Generated Works', https://www.jdsupra.com/legalnews/windows-into-the-future-new-horizons-8432147/ [Accessed 10 January 2025].

Fierberg, Ruthie (2023) 'League of Live Stream Theater Launched by Two Theater and Tech Entrepreneurs', *Broadway News*, 6 January, https://www.broadwaynews.com/league-of-live-stream-theater-launched-by-two-theater-and-tech-entrepreneurs [Accessed 30 May 2024].

Floch, Yohann (2024) 'Foreword', In *Cultural Mobility Flows: Mental Health, Well-Being and International Cultural Mobility: Report and Policy Recommendations*, p 3, https://on-the-move.org/sites/default/files/2024-10/OTM_CMF-Report_Well-being.pdf [Accessed 10 January 2025].

Future Stage Research Group (2021) 'A Manifesto for the Future Stage: Performance Is a Human Right', *American Theatre,* 21 November, https://www.americantheatre.org/2021/11/05/a-manifesto-for-the-future-stage-performance-is-a-human-right/ [Accessed 4 February 2024].

Gardner, Lyn (2025) 'Rachel Zegler's Balcony Moment Exposes Tensions around Access to Theatre', *The Stage*, 23 June, https://www.thestage.co.uk/opinion/rachel-zeglers-balcony-moment-exposes-tensions-around-access-to-theatre-lyn-gardner-evita-jamie-lloyd? [Accessed 30 June 2025].

Gelt, Jessica (2022) '"We're Driving Straight Up the Cliff": Theater Is Back, but Recovery Proves Perilous', *Los Angeles Times,* 11 May, https://www.latimes.com/entertainment-arts/story/2022-05-11/theater-is-back-attendance-is-down-costs-soaring-covid-19-pandemic [Accessed 7 February 2024].

Goldstein, Michael (2022) 'Why Are So Many Broadway Shows Closing?', *Forbes,* 4 October, https://www.forbes.com/sites/michaelgoldstein/2022/10/04/is-fear-of-crime-one-reason-so-many-broadway-shows-are-closing/?sh=1e4939e138ac [Accessed 7 February 2024].

Google Press Center (2008, 1 November) 'Copyright Accord Would Make Millions More Books Available Online', https://googlepress.blogspot.com/2008/10/authors-publishers-and-google-reach_28.html [Accessed 20 October 2024].

Green, Jesse (2024) 'Review: In "Russian Troll Farm," You Can't Stop the Memes', *New York Times,* 8 February, https://www.nytimes.com/2024/02/08/theater/russian-troll-farm-review.html [Accessed 7 February 2024].

Hall, Nate (2022) 'The Show Must Go On: Broadway Theater Struggles to Recover from the Pandemic', *The Tufts Daily*, 24 October, https://www.tuftsdaily.com/article/2022/10/the-show-must-go-on-broadway-theater-struggles-to-recover-from-the-pandemic [Accessed 7 February 2024].

Harpur, Paul (2017) *Discrimination, Copyright and Equality: Opening the E-Book for the Print-Disabled*, Cambridge University Press.

Harpur, Paul and Stein, Michael Ashley (2021) 'The Relevance of the CRPD and Marrakesh Treaty to the Global South', in Michael Ashley Stein and Jonathan Lazar (eds) *Accessible Technology and the Developing World*, Oxford University Press, pp 193–214.

Harpur, Paul, Stein, Michael Ashley, and Ncube, Caroline D. (2023) 'South African Constitutional Court Prioritises Constitutional Right to Access Information by Print Disabled over Protected Copyright Interests', *European Intellectual Property Review* 45(5): 299–305.

Hawthorne, Katie and European Theatre Convention (2023, May) 'Digital Theatre – Digital Strategies and Business Models in European Theatre', https://www.europeantheatre.eu/page/resources/online-library?mc_cid=6334ecc9fb&mc_eid=07cf6a01e3#84 [Accessed 5 February 2024].

Hemley, Matthew (2024) 'Industry-Wide Standards around Disabled Theatregoing Set to Be Rolled Out', *The Stage*, 9 September, https://www.thestage.co.uk/news/industry-wide-standards-around-disabled-theatregoing-set-to-be-rolled-out [Accessed 10 January 2024].

Ilczuk, Dorota, Karpińska, Anna, Cholewicka, Emilia, Piwowar, Kuba, and Socha, Ziemowit (2021) *Artystki i artyści teatru w czasach COVID-19*, Instytut Teatralny, https://www.instytut-teatralny.pl/wp-content/uploads/2021/03/artystki-i-artysci-teatru-w-czasach-covid-19.pdf [Accessed 9 November 2025].

Indigo Ltd (2025) 'Access Culture', https://www.indigo-ltd.com/share/hot-topic/access-cultur [Accessed 27 March 2025].

Infor (2024) 'Tantiemy dla twórców', *Infor*, 14 May, https://www.infor.pl/prawo/nowosci-prawne/6606069,tantiemy-dla-tworcow-za-udostepnianie-ich-dziel-w-internecie-nowelizacja-prawa-autorskiego-przyjeta-przez-rzad-co-sie-zmieni.html [Accessed 30 May 2024].

Iskander, Tarek (2020) 'The Arts After Covid-19: Let's Fix the Things That Weren't Right Before', *The Stage*, 23 April, https://www.thestage.co.uk/opinion/the-arts-after-covid-19-lets-fix-the-things-that-werent-right-before [Accessed 15 February 2024].

Jackson, Maria Rosario and National Endowment for the Arts (2023, October) 'Arts Participation Patterns in 2022: Highlights from the Survey of Public Participation in the Arts', https://www.arts.gov/impact/research/publications/arts-participation-patterns-2022-highlights-survey-public-participation-arts [Accessed 4 February 2024].

Johnson, Eric E. (2010) 'Intellectual Property's Need for a Disability Perspective', *George Mason University Civil Rights Law Journal* 20(2): 181–208.

Kalinowska, Katarzyna, Kułakowska, Katarzyna, Bargielski, Michał, Buchner, Anna, and Wierzbicka, Maria (2021) *Pracownice i pracownicy teatrów w pandemii*, Instytut Teatralny, https://www.instytut-teatralny.pl/wp-content/uploads/2021/04/instytut-teatralny-raport-pracownice-i-pracownicy-teatrow-w-pandemii.pdf [Accessed 9 November 2025].

Kaplan, Jeff (2011) 'In-Library eBook Lending Program Launched', Internet Archive Blog, https://blog.archive.org/2011/02/22/in-library-ebook-lending-program-launched/ [Accessed 20 October 2024].

Kietlińska, Bogna (2021) *Kiedy skończy się kwarantanna i będzie można wrócić do teatru, ja wrócę,: Raport z badania publiczności teatralnej w czasie epidemii koronawirusa w Polsce.* Instutut Teatralny, https://www.instytut-teatralny.pl/wp-content/uploads/2021/04/instytut-teatralny-raport-kiedy-skonczy-sie-kwarantanna-i-bedzie-mozna-wrocic-do-teatru-ja-wroce.pdf [Accessed 9 November 2025].

Klich, Rosemary and Rowson, James (2022) *Theatres beyond the Stage: The Recovery of Regional Theatres as Placemakers in the East of England*, Project Report, University of Essex, https://repository.essex.ac.uk/33674/ [Accessed 5 February 2024].

Knibbs, Kate (2024) 'The Internet Archive Loses Its Appeal of a Major Copyright Case', *Wired*, 4 September, https://www.wired.com/story/internet-archive-loses-hachette-books-case-appeal/ [Accessed 10 January 2025].

Knibbs, Kate (2025) 'Thomson Reuters Wins First Major AI Copyright Case in the US', *Wired*, 11 February, https://www.wired.com/story/thomson-reuters-ai-copyright-lawsuit/ [Accessed 12 February 2025].

Krajewski, Marek and Frąckowiak, Maciej (2021) *W poszukiwaniu strategii: Działania instytucji teatralnych w czasie pandemii*, Instytut Teatralny.

Laney, Douglas B. (2025) 'Copyright or Copywrong? AI's Intellectual Property Conundrum', *Forbes*, 11 February, https://www.forbes.com/sites/douglaslaney/2025/02/11/copyright-or-copywrong-ais-intellectual-property-paradox/ [Accessed 15 February 2025].

Lech, Kasia (2020) 'Lockdown Verses and Anxieties of Presence: How Polish Theatre Rhymed a Case for Its Purpose on the Pandemic Stage', *Critical Stages/Scènes critiques*, December, no 22, https://www.critical-stages.org/22/lockdown-verses-and-anxieties-of-presence-how-polish-theatre-rhymed-a-case-for-its-purpose-on-the-pandemic-stage/ [Accessed 4 April 2024].

Lee, Haimin (2019, October 17) '15 Years of Google Books', https://blog.google/products/search/15-years-google-books/ [Accessed 20 October 2024].

Leguina, Adrian, Manninen, Kadja, and Misek, Richard (2023) 'Beyond the "Substitution Effect": The Impact of Digital Experience Quality on Future Cultural Participation', *Cultural Trends* 34(1), https://doi.org/10.1080/09548963.2023.2295883 [Accessed 23 April 2024].

Lewis, David John (2014) 'Digital Revolution', *Baseline Magazine Blog*, 11 July, https://baselinemagazineblog.wordpress.com/2014/07/11/digital-revolution/ [Accessed 4 February 2024].

Live Performance Australia Guide (2011) 'Arts Access Information Kit', https://liveperformance.com.au/wp-content/uploads/2019/03/LPA-Guide-Arts-Access-Information-Kit.pdf [Accessed 13 February 2024].

Loeppky, John (2021) 'Taking ADA from the Page to the Stage', *American Theatre*, 26 March, https://www.americantheatre.org/2021/03/26/taking-ada-from-the-page-to-the-stage/ [Accessed 4 February 2024].

Luckhurst, Georgia (2024a) 'Academics Warn of "World Without Shakespeare" as Universities Slash Arts', *The Stage*, 26 March, https://www.thestage.co.uk/news/academics-warn-of-world-without-shakespeare-as-universities-slash-arts [Accessed 11 April 2024].

Luckhurst, Georgia (2024b) 'First-Time Theatregoers Made Up More Than Half of 2023 Audiences – Report', *The Stage*, 5 March, https://www.thestage.co.uk/news/first-time-theatregoers-made-up-more-than-half-of-2023-audiences--report [Accessed 11 April 2024].

Luckhurst, Georgia (2024c) 'Theatre Workers "Feel More Hope about Careers Than Screen Employees"', *The Stage*, 19 July, https://www.thestage.co.uk/news/theatre-workers-feel-more-hope-about-careers-than-screen-employees--report [Accessed 27 July 2024].

Mahari, Robert, Fjeld, Jessica, and Epstein, Ziv (2023) 'Generative AI Is a Minefield for Copyright Law', *The Conversation*, 15 June, https://theconversation.com/generative-ai-is-a-minefield-for-copyright-law-207473 [Accessed 9 March 2024].

Marshall, Lisa (2024) '"An Epidemic of Loneliness": How the Pandemic Changed Life for Aging Adults', *CU Boulder Today*, 9 April, https://www.colorado.edu/today/2024/04/09/epidemic-loneliness-how-pandemic-changed-life-aging-adults [Accessed 12 April 2024].

Masso, Giverny (2020) 'Kwame Kwei-Armah: Filming Costs Must Be Hard-Wired into Show Budgets Post-Covid', *The Stage*, 11 June, https://www.thestage.co.uk/news/news/kwame-kwei-armah-filming-costs-must-be-hard-wired-into-show-budgets-post-covid [Accessed 5 February 2024].

metaLAB (at) Harvard (2021) 'FutureStage Manifesto', https://mlml.io/p/futurestage/ [Accessed 4 February 2024].

Misek, Richard, Leguina, Adrian, and Manninen, Kadja (2022) *Digital Access to Arts and Culture*, Arts and Humanities Research Council, https://digiaccessarts.org/report/ [Accessed 4 February 2024].

Morris, Eric A., Speroni, Samuel, and Taylor, Brian D. (2024) 'Going Nowhere Faster: Did the Covid-19 Pandemic Accelerate the Trend Toward Staying Home?', *Journal of the American Planning Association* 91(3): 361–79, https://doi.org/10.1080/01944363.2024.2385327 [Accessed 8 January 2025].

National Academies of Sciences, Engineering, and Medicine (2020) *Social Isolation and Loneliness in Older Adults: Opportunities for the Health Care System*, National Academies Press, https://doi.org/10.17226/25663 [Accessed 22 July 2024].

National Endowment for the Arts (2023, December) *Online Audiences for Arts Programming: A Survey of Virtual Participation amid COVID-19*, https://www.arts.gov/impact/research/publications/online-audiences-arts-programming-survey-virtual-participation-amid-covid-19 [Accessed 4 February 2024].

National Endowment for the Arts Office of Accessibility (2010) '2010 Revised Regulations of the American with Disabilities Act Titles II and III', https://www.arts.gov/sites/default/files/NEA-ADA-TipSheet-v2.pdf [Accessed 27 April 2024].

National Library Service for the Blind and Print Disabled (nd-a) 'Eligibility for Individual Service', Library of Congress, https://www.loc.gov/nls/how-to-enroll/apply-for-nls-services/#eligibility-guidelines [Accessed 12 November 2024].

National Library Service for the Blind and Print Disabled (nd-b) 'History', Library of Congress, https://www.loc.gov/nls/who-we-are/history/ [Accessed 12 November 2024].

Ncube, Caroline B., Reid, Blake E., and Oriakhogba, Desmond O. (2020) 'Beyond the Marrakesh VIP Treaty: Typology of Copyright Access-Enabling Provisions for Persons with Disabilities', *The Journal of World Intellectual Property* 23(3–4): 149–65, https://doi.org/10.1111/jwip.12144 [Accessed 28 July 2024].

NESTA (2011) 'NT Live: Digital Broadcast of Theatre – Learning from the Pilot Season', http://www.nesta.org.uk/library/documents/NTLive_web.pdf [Accessed 12 November 2013].

Norris, Rufus (2024) 'What We've Learned from 100 NY Live Productions', *The Stage*, 23 April, https://www.thestage.co.uk/opinion/what-weve-learned-from-100-nt-live-productions-rufus-norris [Accessed 23 November 2024].

Okundaye, Jason (2024) 'My Hunt for a Missing TV Episode – And What it Shows about Being Black in Britain', *The Guardian*, 13 May, https://www.theguardian.com/commentisfree/article/2024/may/13/tv-episode-black-britain-gay-history?s=09 [Accessed 31 May 2024].

On The Move (2021) 'Time to Act: How Lack of Knowledge in the Cultural Sector Creates Barriers for Disabled Artists and Audiences', https://www.ietm.org/en/resources/reports/time-to-act-how-lack-of-knowledge-in-the-cultural-sector-creates-barriers-for-0 [Accessed 4 February 2024].

Orland, Kyle (2024) 'Can an Online Library of Classic Video Games Ever Be Legal?', *Ars Technica*, 25 April, https://arstechnica.com/gaming/2024/04/can-an-online-library-of-classic-video-games-ever-be-legal/?s=09 [Accessed 30 May 2024].

Ostrower, Francie and the Wallace Foundation (2024) 'In Search of a Magic Bullet: Results from the Building Audiences for Sustainability Initiative', https://wallacefoundation.org/sites/default/files/2024-02/in-search-of-the-magic-bullet-results-form-building-audiences-for-sustainability-initiative.pdf [Accessed 4 April 2024].

Parker, Amanda (2024) 'What Does Kwame Kwei-Armah's Departure Tell Us about Arts Leadership Today?', *The Stage*, 9 February, https://www.thestage.co.uk/opinion/what-does-kwame-kwei-armahs-departure-tell-us-about-arts-leadership-today#:~:text=Kwei%2DArmah's%20departure%20highlights%20much,office%20as%20advance%20bookings%20dwindle [Accessed 10 April 2024].

Paulson, Michael and Hernández, Javier C. (2022) 'Live Performance Is Back. But Audiences Have Been Slow to Return', *New York Times*, 22 August, https://www.nytimes.com/2022/08/21/arts/performing-arts-pandemic-attendance.html [Accessed 7 February 2024].

Peach, Jasper (2022) 'Australia's Return to Live Performance Is Triumphant – But So Many of Us Are Being Left Behind', *The Guardian*, 28 September, https://www.theguardian.com/commentisfree/2022/oct/06/the-end-to-mandatory-covid-isolation-is-a-gut-punch-for-medically-vulnerable-australians [Accessed 7 February 2024].

Peters, Jens (2014) 'The National Theatre Goes International: Global Branding and the Regions', in Magda Romanska (ed) *The Routledge Companion to Dramaturgy*, Routledge, pp 124–9.

Reid, Blake Ellis (2021) 'Copyright and Disability', *California Law Review* 109(19–16): 2172–223, https://www.californialawreview.org/print/copyright-and-disability [Accessed 25 April 2024].

Ritter, Ian (2025) 'Brown, Trinity Indefinitely Pause Admissions to MFA Program', *Brown Daily Herald*, 29 January, https://www.browndailyherald.com/article/2025/01/brown-trinity-indefinitely-pause-admissions-to-mfa-program [Accessed 12 February 2025].

Romanska, Magda (2012) *The Post-Traumatic Theatre of Grotowski and Kantor*, Anthem Press.

Romanska, Magda (ed) (2014) *The Routledge Companion to Dramaturgy*, Routledge.

Romanska, Magda (2021) 'Envisioning Your Art, Post Pandemic', *ArtSake*, 15 July, https://artsake.massculturalcouncil.org/envisioning-your-art-post-pandemic/ [Accessed 4 February 2024].

Romanska, Magda, and Lech, Kasia (2024) 'TheTheatreTimes.com: Towards Transnational Digital Infrastructure', *The Theatre Times*, 27 January, https://thetheatretimes.com/thetheatretimes-com-towards-transnational-digital-infrastructure [Accessed 20 June 2024].

Ruhl, Sarah (2024) 'All the Lonely People: We Say Theatre Can Be Healing, but What If That Were Literally True?', *American Theatre*, 7 June, https://www.americantheatre.org/2024/06/07/all-the-lonely-people/ [Accessed 12 June 2024].

Salvador, Phil (2024, 25 October) 'Statement on the DMCA 2024 Triennial Review Ruling', https://gamehistory.org/dmca-2024-statement/ [Accessed 15 December 2024].

Schechner, Richard (1977) *Performance Theory*, Routledge.

Schechner, Richard (1985) *Between Theater and Anthropology*, University of Pennsylvania Press.

Schrader, Adam (2025) 'How This A.I. Image Became the First to Snag Copyright Protection', *Artnet*, 12 February, https://news.artnet.com/art-world/invoke-snags-first-ai-image-copyright-2608219 [Accessed 15 February 2025].

Shaw, Helen (2025) 'The Show Can't Go On', *New Yorker*, 24 April, https://www.newyorker.com/news/the-lede/the-show-cant-go-on [Accessed 26 April 2025].

Shumailov, Ilia, Shumaylov, Z., Zhao, Y., Papernot, N., Anderson, R., and Gal, Y. (2024) 'AI Models Collapse When Trained on Recursively Generated Data', *Nature* 631(8022): 755–9, https://doi.org/10.1038/s41586-024-07566-y [Accessed 21 October 2024].

Silber, Bohne, Silber & Associates, and Triplett, Tim, The Urban Institute (2015) *A Decade of Arts Engagement: Findings from the Survey of Public Participation in the Arts, 2002–2012*, National Endowment for the Arts, https://www.arts.gov/sites/default/files/2012-sppa-feb2015.pdf [Accessed 4 April 2024].

Smith, Alistair (2024) 'Sonia Friedman Is Right – Theatre's Sea Change Can Be an Opportunity', *The Stage*, 15 February, https://www.thestage.co.uk/opinion/sonia-friedman-is-right—theatres-sea-change-can-be-an-opportunity [Accessed 15 February 2024].

Smith, Kimberley J., Gavey, S., Riddell, Natalie E., Kontari, P., and Victor, C. (2020) 'The Association between Loneliness, Social Isolation and Inflammation: A Systematic Review and Meta-Analysis', *Neuroscience & Biobehavioral Reviews* 112: 519–41, https://doi.org/10.1016/j.neubiorev.2020.02.002 [Accessed 29 July 2024].

Societies and Cultures Institute (2024) 'Pandemic Preparedness in the Live Performing Arts: Lessons to Learn from Covid-19 in the G7 Countries. Project Report', University of Exeter, https://www.exeter.ac.uk/v8media/research/sci/Pandemic_Preparedness_G7LitReviews.pdf [Accessed 4 May 2024].

Spangler, Todd (2022) 'Netflix Plans to Expand Audio Descriptions, Subtitling in More Than 10 Additional Languages', *Variety*, 19 May, https://variety.com/2022/digital/news/netflix-expand-audio-descriptions-subtitling-languages-1235271343/ [Accessed 21 October 2024].

Sperling, Nicole (2024) 'Audience Snapshot: Four Years after Shutdown, a Mixed Recovery', *New York Times*, 12 March, https://www.nytimes.com/2024/03/12/arts/covid-shutdown-live-audiences.html [Accessed 11 April 2024].

Stevens, Matt (2023) 'Brooklyn Academy of Music Lays Off 13 Percent of Its Staff', *New York Times*, 26 June, https://www.nytimes.com/2023/06/26/theater/brooklyn-academy-of-music-layoffs.html [Accessed 7 February 2024].

Szulczynski, Wojciech (1996) 'Review: "Forefather's Eve": Twelve Improvisations"', *Theatre Journal* 48(4, December): 499–503.

Taylor, Diana (2003) *The Archive and the Repertoire: Performing Cultural Memory in the Americas*, Duke University Press, https://doi.org/10.2307/j.ctv11smz1k [Accessed 4 February 2024].

Teachout, Terry (2013) 'How Theatres Can Combat the Stay-at-Home Mindset', *Wall Street Journal*, 25 December, http://online.wsj.com/news/articles/SB10001424052702304866904579266882201324884 [Accessed 25 December 2013].

*Theater: Digital Dramaturgies* 42(2, 2012), https://www.dukeupress.edu/digital-feelings [Accessed 4 February 2024].

*Theater: Digital Feelings* 46(2, 2016), https://www.dukeupress.edu/digital-feelings [Accessed 4 February 2024].

Thorpe, Vanessa (2023) 'Exit, Pursued by Stress: Bosses of Smaller UK Theatres Quit in Droves', *The Guardian*, 13 August, https://www.theguardian.com/stage/2023/aug/13/worry-as-uk-theatre-bosses-quit-in-droves [Accessed 11 April 2024].

Todorut, Ilinca (2016) 'Christina Papagiannouli on Cyberformance, Online Theatre and Pokémon GO', *The Theatre Times*, 3 August, https://thetheatretimes.com/christina-papagiannouli-cyberformance-online-theatre-pokemon-go [Accessed 4 February 2024].

Tompkins, Joanna (2023) 'The Digital Turn: Research and Publishing in Theatre Journal', *Theatre Journal* 75(4): 425–36, https://doi.org/10.1353/tj.2023.a922213 [Accessed 22 July 2024].

Trueman, Matt (2013) 'The Surprise Success of NT Live', *The Guardian*, 9 June.

Tymicki, Jerzy and Niezgoda, Andrzej (1986) 'New Dignity: The Polish Theatre 1970–1985', *TDR: The Drama Review* 30(3, Autumn): 13–46.

United Kingdom Government (2010) 'Equality Act 2010, Section 15', https://www.legislation.gov.uk/ukpga/2010/15/section/15 [Accessed 13 February 2024].

United Kingdom Government (2023, 5 October) 'Accessibility and Assisted Digital: Making Your Service Accessible: An Introduction', https://www.gov.uk/service-manual/helping-people-to-use-your-service/making-your-service-accessible-an-introduction#:~:text=Your%20service%20must%20be%20accessible,you%20design%20or%20build%20anything [Accessed 13 February 2024].

United Kingdom, the Copyright, Designs and Patents Act 1988 (CDPA) Sections 31A–31F (2014) 'Disabled Person: Copies of Works for Personal Use', https://www.legislation.gov.uk/ukpga/1988/48/section/31A/2014-06-01 [Accessed 24 April 2024].

United Kingdom Intellectual Property Office (2014/2021) 'Details of the Exceptions to Copyright That Allow Limited Use of Copyright Works without the Permission of the Copyright Owner', https://www.gov.uk/guidance/exceptions-to-copyright#helping-disabled-people [Accessed 28 April 2024].

United Nations (1948, 10 December) 'Universal Declaration of Human Rights': Article 27, https://www.ohchr.org/en/press-releases/2018/12/universal-declaration-human-rights-70-30-articles-30-articles-article-27#:~:text=Article%2027%20says%20everyone%20has,as%20human%20rights%20for%20all [Accessed 4 February 2024].

United Nations, General Assembly resolution 2200A (XXI) (1966a, 16 December) 'International Covenant on Civil and Political Rights', https://www.ohchr.org/en/instruments-mechanisms/instruments/international-covenant-civil-and-political-rights [Accessed 4 February 2024].

United Nations, General Assembly resolution 2200A (XXI) (1966b, 16 December) 'International Covenant on Economic, Social and Cultural Rights', https://www.ohchr.org/en/instruments-mechanisms/instruments/international-covenant-economic-social-and-cultural-rights [Accessed 4 February 2024].

United Nations (2007, 24 January) 'United Nations Convention on the Rights of Persons with Disabilities, resolution 61/106 (Article 30, paragraph 3)', https://www.ohchr.org/sites/default/files/Documents/HRBodies/CRPD/CRPD_ENG.pdf [Accessed 4 February 2024].

United Nations Department of Economic and Social Affairs (nd) 'Factsheet on Persons with Disabilities', https://www.un.org/development/desa/disabilities/resources/factsheet-on-persons%20-with-disabilities.html [Accessed 26 April 2024].

United States, 118th Congress, 2nd Session (2024) 'Supporting Theater and the Arts to Galvanize the Economy (STAGE) Act of 2024', https://www.welch.senate.gov/wp-content/uploads/2024/04/STAGE-Act-FINAL_Welch_Fetterman_Reed.pdf [Accessed 28 April 2024].

United States Copyright Office (2024) 'Exemption to Prohibition on Circumvention of Copyright Protection Systems for Access Control Technologies (37 CFR Part 201) [Final rule]', *Federal Register*, 28 October, p 8, https://www.federalregister.gov/documents/2024/10/28/2024-24563/exemption-to-prohibition-on-circumvention-of-copyright-protection-systems-for-access-control [Accessed 28 October 2024].

United States Copyright Office (2025) 'Copyright and Artificial Intelligence', https://www.copyright.gov/ai/Copyright-and-Artificial-Intelligence-Part-2-Copyrightability-Report.pdf [Accessed 12 February 2025].

Vasan, Shradha, Eikelis, Nina, Lim, Michelle H., and Lambert, Elisabeth (2023) 'Evaluating the Impact of Loneliness and Social Isolation on Health Literacy and Health-Related Factors in Young Adults', *Frontiers in Psychology* 14, Article 996611, https://doi.org/10.3389/fpsyg.2023.996611 [Accessed 22 July 2024].

Vincentelli, Elisabeth (2021) '"chekhovOS /an experimental game" Review: Life on a Merry-Go-Round', *New York Times*, 31 May, https://www.nytimes.com/2021/05/31/theater/chekhovos-an-experimental-game-review.html [Accessed 20 June 2024].

Vaughan, Jane (2023) 'How the Oregon Shakespeare Festival's Financial Troubles Became So Serious', *OPB*, June 18, https://www.opb.org/article/2023/06/18/oregon-shakespeare-festival-financial-troubles-analysis/ [Accessed 7 February 2024].

Willman, Chris (2023) 'Mark Taper Forum Cancels All Productions Planned for 2023–24 Season, Due to "Crisis Unlike Any Other in Our 56-Year History"', *Variety*, 15 June, https://variety.com/2023/legit/news/mark-taper-forum-cancels-productions-season-center-theatre-group-cutbacks-1235646230/ [Accessed 7 February 2024].

World Health Organization (WHO) (2018, February 21) 'Disability (Factsheet)', https://www.who.int/news-room/facts-in-pictures/detail/disabilities [Accessed 28 July 2024].

World Intellectual Property Organization (WIPO) (2012) 'Beijing Treaty on Audiovisual Performances', https://www.wipo.int/treaties/en/ip/beijing/ [Accessed 28 April 2024].

World Intellectual Property Organization (WIPO) (2013a) 'Marrakesh Treaty to Facilitate Access to Published Works for Persons Who Are Blind, Visually Impaired or Otherwise Print Disabled', https://www.wipo.int/treaties/en/ip/marrakesh/ [Accessed 28 April 2024].

World Intellectual Property Organization (WIPO) (2013b) 'Summary of the Marrakesh Treaty to Facilitate Access to Published Works for Persons Who Are Blind, Visually Impaired, or Otherwise Print Disabled (MVT)', https://www.wipo.int/treaties/en/ip/marrakesh/summary_marrakesh.html [Accessed 28 April 2024].

World Intellectual Property Organization (WIPO) (2022) 'Session on the Impact of the COVID-19 Pandemic on the Copyright Ecosystem – 9 May 2022', https://www.wipo.int/meetings/en/2022/info-session-impact-covid-19-copyright-ecosystems.html [Accessed 13 February 2024].

Yakubovskaya, Irina (2019) '"Art Tells Truth That Truth Itself Can't": A Glimpse into the Multimedia Mind of Schneider', *The Theatre Times*, 26 April, https://thetheatretimes.com/art-tells-truth-that-truth-itself-cant-a-glimpse-into-the-multimedia-mind-of-andrew-schneider/ [Accessed 4 February 2024].

ZASP (2023) 'Tantiemy', https://www.zasp.pl/ozz/tantiemy/liczenie-tantiem/ [Accessed 30 May 2024].

# Index

References to notes show both the page number and the note number (122n49).

## C



## D

Printed and bound by CPI Group (UK) Ltd, Croydon, CR0 4YY
15/09/2026
14962386-0002